Life After the Mistake

By Sheila Textor

Copyright © 2021 by Bee Ministries, Sheila Textor.
All rights reserved. No part of this book may be reproduced, transmitted, or distributed in any form or by electronic means without prior written permission of the publisher, except in the form of short quotations for book reviews and certain other noncommercial uses permitted by copyright law.

This is a work of creative non-fiction. All of the events in this memoir are true to the best of the author's memory. Some names and identifying features have been changed to protect the identity of certain parties. The author in no way represents any company, corporation, or brand, mentioned herein. The views expressed in this memoir are solely those of the author.

All scriptures in this book are taken from the King James Version (KJV) of the Bible, which exists in the public domain in the United States.

ISBN
Paperback: 978-1-7361575-3-4
Ebook: 978-1-7361575-4-1

Independently published by Bee Ministries, Sheila Textor.
Blytheville, Arkansas

Second edition, 2021.

Front cover design by: Theresa Mainers
Edited by: April Jones
Book designed and edited by: Sinclaire Sparkman

YouTube: Bee Ministries

Life After the Mistake

By Sheila Textor

Contents

Foreword 7

Introduction 8

Part 1: The Mistake 11
Chapter 1: Kings Still Fall 13
Chapter 2: Good People Fall 19
Chapter 3: Broken Beginnings 25
Chapter 4: Hard Middles 29
Chapter 5: Hoping For Nothing 33
Chapter 6: The Trap Is Set 37
Chapter 7: Hope Turns 41
Chapter 8: A Place To Begin Again 45
Chapter 9: When Home Feels Unfamiliar 51
Chapter 10: When Healing Is In The Air 57

Part 2: A Different Set Of Eyes 61
The Betrayer 63
The Betrayed 68

A Different Set Of Eyes 74
Stories From The Bible 74
The Appointment For Grace 75
The Very Act 79
The Widow's Garment 83
The Road To New Beginnings 86

Part 3: New Beginnings 92
Chapter 1: A New Path 95
Chapter 2: The Job Had To Go 99
Chapter 3: Knocking On Doors 103

Chapter 4: Shadows 109
Chapter 5: My Journal 115
Chapter 6: No C-Section Callings 119
Chapter 7: Seasons 123
Chapter 8: The Word 131
Chapter 9: The Building 135
Chapter 10: The Calling 143
Chapter 11: The Move 149

The Journey Continues 153

Acknowledgments 154

Foreword

While there are many books available for those looking to self-improve or grow closer in their walk with God, I dare to say there are few that brave the topic of a comeback to God's army after we have fallen victim to the temptation of sin.

The author, Mrs. Textor, embraces sharing the uncomfortable and yet all too familiar scenario of infidelity, especially infidelity in the church, in this first book of her new series, Life After The Mistake. Satan will tempt you wherever he can and when we are tricked, the climb back to our calling can be a slippery slope even though God's forgiveness is granted.

When moving on is often done by burying the memory and never mentioning it again, digging up these dry bones in this book is an incredible reminder of how we continue to face spiritual warfare in our journey as Christians even when we try diligently to steer clear of temptation, trials, and sin, and how trying to fix it and forget it ourselves is not nearly as powerful as following God's direction toward resolve and being willing to do whatever He asks us to do regardless of how difficult or uncomfortable it may be.

By combining Biblical truths and examples with a present day dilemma, this book allows an opportunity for you to gain a new perspective regardless of your part in the aftermath of sin.

With her authenticity and humility, this story will be one you won't want to put down and will leave you with renewed hope in a future of forgiveness for yourself and others, reparation of relationships that you may not have imagined possible, and a life of joy pursuing God's calling for you, regardless of your past mistakes.

—Dr. April Jones, author of No Mess No Message and Cofounder of The Drifted Drum Co.

Introduction

I love to hear the stories of how God delivered someone from drugs, alcohol, street gangs, prison, and even from the desire to commit suicide. People who have been through these things often have testimonies of near death experiences or how God intervened for them in a supernatural way. And while these testimonies are impactful and worthy of sharing, this book will not be sharing those stories. In this book, we are going to explore stories of Christians who fell from grace after they came to know the Lord.

Not everyone can relate to these stories, and if you have never failed God in the manner these people have, then I definitely am so thankful for your witness in the Christian walk. But as you read here, you will see how some of the greatest people in the Bible and in our generation have let God down, as well as their families and their spouses. These believers let their guards down and fell into worst-case scenarios.

I am sharing these stories to encourage those who have allowed sin to overtake them and can't seem to recover from the damage it has caused. The goal is not to excuse this ugly sin, but to acknowledge it happened and to recognize that it happens to fellow Christians more often than we like to realize. Yes, this sin I am referring to is the one that starts with A: Adultery.

Since you have this book in your hand, you may have either been at fault or maybe your family has fallen victim to adultery's vices, or perhaps you haven't yet made the mistake but are being tempted.

This book contains answers to hard questions and will help you see the light of day, no matter where you are in this journey. These are real stories from real people who have walked this road, and some are still recovering. I must tell you that even King David never lived it down; the Bible tells us that it was ever before him. One thing is for sure, though, life goes on and forgiveness is there for you. God is in the restoration business. All you have to do is be willing to be restored. He won't withhold His love from you because of a mistake.

Part 1: The Mistake

Psalm 51:1-3

Have mercy upon me, O God, according to thy lovingkindness: according unto the multitude of thy tender mercies blot out my transgressions.

Wash me throughly from mine iniquity, and cleanse me from my sin.

For I acknowledge my transgressions: and my sin is ever before me.

Chapter 1: Kings Still Fall

There she was, bathing right out in the open, and beautiful to look upon from what the Bible says about Bathsheba. King David saw her from his rooftop, and from that view in that moment their world would start a downhill journey. What is it about our natural eye that keeps humans in trouble so much?

Maybe it can be traced back to the Garden of Eden. It is there that Eve was deceived because she wanted what her eyes could see but she knew was forbidden. Even in that perfect setting, there was an undercurrent of curiosity that caused Eve to carry on a conversation with the Enemy. Is our humanness always to blame for our desire to cross the line? We have guidelines that we follow; there are lines that shouldn't be crossed. Temptation has always been there, but God gives us the antidote.

As David gazed upon Bathsheba's naked body, the other kings were out in battle, but David had stayed home. He was already out of place. He should have been out with the other kings, battling. Wrong place. Wrong time. Yet it was so easy to do what his flesh wanted to do. There was no pondering on the decision about what he wanted. He tells the guards to bring her to him.

He does the unthinkable, even though he was told that she was married. His lust was stronger than his conviction.

Then one fall leads to another fall. Bathsheba became pregnant. David arranged for her husband to be killed in battle. A pregnant woman, a murdered soldier, and a lifetime of heartache and problems would all be linked to this failure. King David caused his bloodline to suffer so much pain that we find him in Psalms weeping and repenting in many chapters. For this failure he paid a significant cost. But David exhibits recovery after sin.

King David did not get removed from his position nor did he lose his anointing. Am I making excuses for this behavior? No. But David was still called by God for a purpose, and God was still going to use him.

I want to help you see beyond the fall, the ugly mistake, the harvest from the seed you sowed, if you let me. I am well aware of the consequences that come with this mistake. But while the act of adultery is going on, people rarely consider the possible consequences. Once they have given in to sin, the Devil has them deceived into thinking that somehow, despite their actions, everything will be okay. The Bible tells us the punishment for David was heartbreaking from the very beginning. He loses the child that was conceived in this act of sin. Much bloodshed was in this family, even with his own sons. He knew God could have killed him and replaced him.

David felt condemned and was quick to repent. This was the key that would help him regain his footing: repenting, with all his heart. That is our key, too, no matter how bad it was or how far it went, God has made a way for each of us to ask for forgiveness. When we truly repent, being sorry for our actions, we can begin the process of restoration. Like clay on the Potter's wheel, we can be reshaped or redone to be used in the Master's plan.

So many people have allowed their mistakes to keep them from walking in the calling that God has for them. The Bible tells us that our gifts and callings are without repentance. Whatever God has called you to do, you cannot walk away from it. Yes, there are consequences. Will you always be remembered for the act? More than likely, you will. Will your sin ever be before your eyes? Yes, I can attest it will. Just ask David. Nonetheless, my dear friends, life doesn't have to be centered on any mistake that we have made. Our Heavenly Father can and will pick you up and put you in good standing with Him and man again.

Sometimes we wonder how we can find ourselves in such a place, looking back is always different than when it is happening. There is pleasure in sin for a season. Just living for those fleeting moments keeps us longer than we intend and costs us more than we could ever afford, like years of shame, guilt, distrust, and a marred reputation.

I'm not going to leave you without a remedy. God is there to help you. He is there with his love, mercy, and grace. You are not alone; He was there when you were looking at that forbidden fruit. He was there when you were being led astray. He was still reaching out for you. He didn't want you to fail or fall. People often want to just move on and bury the awful failure, but perhaps we could learn from it. God will cover the multitude of sins. It's one of his greatest attributes, called God's Love. He wants to restore you.

I've been on both sides of this spectrum. I know what it's like to be so heartbroken that everything feels numb. It's like a movie that you want to end. Everybody else seems to be going on with their lives while yours is standing still. This feeling can be found in almost every tragedy and especially in divorce. You can find life after tragedy, after the fall, after the affair, and yes, even after the divorce.

As my heart goes out to the one who has been hurt, I also feel empathy for the ones who have failed. While many are able to move on post-infidelity, I have met many women within the church who struggle to put the pieces back together. We are not here to pull these sins out from under the blood of Christ. They have been forgiven and thrown into the sea of forgetfulness. Our goal is to get you to do the same. Many people are still locked in their own prison of guilt and shame, reliving the sin over and over while their former co-conspirator in the affair may be able to recover more quickly, getting back to "normal life." Let's get real here; it can be downright frustrating.

Social media can be especially painful. All smiles and anniversaries, and life seems to be going well for them. Sometimes it truthfully is. The feeling you get when you see their happiness may not be a good feeling. That is precisely why I'm writing this book, because my dear sweet friend, I want to keep you from drowning. You may feel hurt, angry, and sometimes even jealous. But God is asking you to let it go. Let go of what was and step into what is. Get your life back, go back to your first love, the love of God. The great heart surgeon has His surgical knife prepared to cut out that lost feeling of hopelessness that you want to get rid of so desperately. God is well aware of all those emotions that are wearing you down. Your inner man is screaming, "Please, unlock the door and let me out."

Time is standing still for no one. Years are passing you by. Get that excited, joyous feeling back in your life. Truly start living again, more than just going through the motions. You may have a job. You may have stayed in your marriage. You might even still go to church regularly. (Oh yes, the Church. We will address that in the next few chapters.) But it's common that you may not feel "normal," you may not feel happy, and you may have not yet recovered.

"The greatest king of Israel, King David, the author of Psalms, sent a man out to die in battle so he could sleep with his wife."
-Robert Duvall

1 Corinthians 10:12
Wherefore let him that thinketh he standeth take heed lest he fall.

Chapter 2: Good People Fall

Churches are full of broken people. People in church have fallen into the trap of infidelity. Some fell on purpose, while others were caught off guard by this age-old sin that has taken many good men and women down paths of destruction. We all have sinned and came up short. Perhaps you are the one that fell, or you are the one that got hurt, but either way, if you have been hurt by adultery, this book is here to help.

When it comes to sexual sin, we are all victims in some way or another. I know from experience how participating in this act can leave you ashamed and empty. At first, you may think it's okay. Oh the feelings that can get in you, they feel so real at the time. You almost feel that you're justified, but this is the plot of the enemy to play on your emotions. The feelings may in fact be real, but emotions are merely information being transmitted through the flesh.

Infidelity cannot be justified. There are no excuses for it. We are in control of our actions, no matter how strong the emotions get. Also, God does not excuse it. And there will always be a harvest from the seeds we have sown. Let's face the facts, it still happens and has happened to the best of people. It's possible to get back up and move on, to keep going despite the wrong.

Often, these failures never get dealt with. The sin might be left in secret because of shame, or if it's found out, merely swept under the rug because of fear or pride. Sometimes, there are consequences for adultery. The offender may have to step down from their position of power in the church for a time. Maybe both parties in the sin are members within the same assembly, and both must be reprimanded in this way or encouraged to separate from interacting even within the confines of the church. While it's not my place to determine punishment for the person or even the severity of the reprimand, I do want to help you forgive yourself, so you can let God heal you and bring complete victory into your life. The fact is, it happened.

Let's get you up so you can dust yourself off and get back in the race. That is easier said than done. I'm writing this book from the view of one who has failed. I fell to the sin of adultery. I went through years of just existing. I had to leave the place that I loved because of my sin. And I had to move on with my life. I eventually got remarried.

I believe my experience in my first marriage had a lot to contribute to my actions after the divorce. In that marriage, I was the victim of adulterous behavior. I was the wife that was neglected, abused, and betrayed. My bitterness jaded my views of marriage. Perhaps it was difficult to weigh the consequences of destroying someone else's home against my own actions when it was finally my turn to make a choice. Even so, I know I was selfish in this act.

So where are you? That's my question. Are you hiding out? Just staying behind the scenes? Are you going through the motions, pretending that you have your life under control? Well, I can probably pull on every string that is hanging from this past failure: every regret, every thought, every longing, and every desire. I understand. I'm here to tell you that you are allowed to be free and do those things that God has called you to do. His grace is that good. God doesn't want to see you in that prison of guilt and shame to which only you hold the key. Some of you may have even allowed this guilt and shame to rob you of the joy of going to church. Don't give the devil the right to stop your life. Now, God is there, waiting for you to cry out to him, waiting on you to allow healing and change. The past cannot hold you any longer. You have to be willing to make steps in the right direction. Your steps may look different than mine, but the main goal is to start stepping.

Go with me on my journey back to God, back to my place. Yes, my place. Not a building, not a town but a place in my heart. There were ghosts in my heart, walls that had me hemmed in. All I can say is that God never left me. The life that I had settled into was my own. It wasn't the life that God had planned for me. My actions led me off track and delayed my destiny. But God allowed time for the dust to settle, and then he was ready to bring things full circle. I was still his child. I was his chosen one. No one could do what he called me to do. I will tell you that when God first started moving me back to my place, it didn't seem like the great big adventure that it is now.

Going back home, especially after being gone for a long period of time, can often be daunting. People at home can remain guarded when you leave because of some foolish mistakes or wrong decisions you made. In counseling sessions, the pastor/therapist/counselor may suggest you return home. Home can be a different place for all of us. Some will have to go back to their hometown, others to their families. And perhaps some must even return to the church.

You cannot heal if you do not face the skeleton that hangs in your heart's closet. Taking those first steps can be very hard, not knowing what lies ahead. Fear, shame, guilt, and regret will absolutely overwhelm your mind. You have to know that sometimes it's not just you who needs to face those ghosts of the past. From my experience, there may be several people that will need this as well as you, and though you are not responsible for what they choose to do, your bravery could lead them to freedom as well.

We need to forgive. They need to forgive. We often just want to make sense of it all. We are talking about failing God and people. This book is centered around affairs, adultery and infidelity, but any failure or mistake can have people pushed up in a corner, making it hard to cope with life. That's why we have to deal with the failures. It could simply be a sincere apology asking for forgiveness. This may take several times and doing something to truly let them know that you are sincere. Don't beat yourself up. Do what you feel like God wants you to do. Be sure and pray much about all involved. Then, leave the rest to God.

Can I tell you that God is for you? He wants to set you free. You are loved and forgiven. He longs to fellowship with you. He misses you. Some of you may be attending churches, even singing on praise teams and participating in the services. Taking action to do the right things is important and noteworthy. But are you just going through the motions? How do you move past just going through the motions?

You truly love the Lord. Your actions are sincere. Only you know the battles that your mind puts you through. I can relate. I'm an overcomer as well. Don't settle for your routine commitments. Thank God for them, but don't settle for the mundane when you can live one of the most fulfilling lives you ever lived. Man can't stop you, maybe hinder you, but never stop you.

**There is a little Humpty Dumpty in us all.
We are humans.**

Jeremiah 17:9
The heart is deceitful above all things, and desperately wicked: who can know it?

Chapter 3: Broken Beginnings

Allow me to share with you the story of Bill and Shelly. This story is based on true events. Some liberties have been taken to fabricate where necessary in regards to supposed feelings of the characters and fine details of events. But overall, the story bears truth about how Satan can catch us when we are weak. But God can restore and repair beyond comprehension.

Let's start with Shelly's journey to this great fall. Shelly married young at the age of 16. She thought she was escaping a life of lack. There was never any real stability in her life. Her mother left this earth before Shelly was 12 years old. From that time on, she was left with family or whoever would let her stay with them. She had no solid role model in her life. She saw things that a young girl shouldn't have had to see. Her father was not in her life enough to make her feel secure about her future.

Shelly didn't think about the future. She quit school at age 14. The emptiness in Shelly's life left her vulnerable to the opposite sex. Her life lacked love and security. At 15, she began to date the man who would become her husband, Rick. Pregnant at 15 was the norm in Shelly's family. Marriage seemed like the perfect escape. Instead, she was in for the ride of her life.

Even before their first child was born, the nightmare that would last the whole marriage had begun. Shelly's husband had been married before, even though he was still a teen himself. His family had told Shelly that Rick abused his first wife. He also betrayed her with other women. When you're 15, sometimes you don't listen, and it's easy to buy in to beliefs that later seem ridiculous.

Shelly thought surely it was the woman's fault. She probably gave him good reasons to cheat on her. No doubt she was the problem or he wouldn't have hit her. With time, she would wish a thousand times over that she would have listened to her instincts instead of her naïve mind.

One day at a gas station, Shelly sat in the truck with Rick's uncle while her then-fiance pumped gas. After the other man was dropped off, the accusing began. What had she done to tempt this man as they sat innocently and casually? His anger and jealousy were real despite being unwarranted. A hard slap across the face was the first of many to come.

Soon, it was the wedding day, and Rick and Shelly said their "I do's" Before God, they promised to love each other in sickness and health, to be faithful, and kind. If only Rick had meant those words, her life could have been very different.

The first few months after they married, Rick and Shelly stayed with Rick's parents. The accusations and physical abuse continued. The things that Shelly had seen in her youth made her feel like this life was reflective of normal married life.

It was quite a big event when they finally moved into their own place as a married couple. Shelly hoped being in their own place would help their relationship and that the atmosphere would experience a positive change. He didn't hit her every day, perhaps weekly, brought on by the occasions of minor disagreements or if an opportunity arose for jealousy (even if it was unfounded). Shelly became insecure and jealous.

Shelly's husband only worked about three minutes

from their new place. On one occasion, the lady next door had brought some left over dinner to Shelly before her husband came home. The ground was covered with snow, and the thoughtful neighbor left footprints on the doorstep. When Rick came home for lunch, he was confident that the tracks were left by her lover coming to steal her hot affection in the middle of the day. Abuse followed, as always.

At this point, Shelly was about seven months pregnant, but the hitting still did not stop. He would strike her across her head or push her around. This particular day he pushed Shelly to the floor. He demanded that she tell him who had been there. He threatened if she didn't have an answer for him by the time he got off from work that evening that she better not be there. Shelly walked to a nearby store and called a family member to come get her.

This would go on for several years.

Shelly carried another great disillusion in her heart that once she was married she would feel complete. She would have a place to call home, a safe place, the security she always needed. This was surely nothing like she had pictured as a little girl watching fantasy love stories. They moved many times, from one place to another, and back in with Rick's parents whenever money was too tight. They would always have to borrow money or food to make it. If it wasn't for her in-laws, she would not have even had a place. They never could keep a car. They were always out of butane, and there was never money for extra things. It was not the fairy tale marriage she had imagined.

Colossians 3:13

Forbearing one another, and forgiving one another, if any man have a quarrel against any: even as Christ forgave you, so also do ye.

Chapter 4: Hard Middles

During those early years of Shelly's marriage, the physical abuse made Shelly feel like something was wrong with her. She often would not say what was in her heart or even speak at all for fear of the abuse. Shelly compared herself to other women that were single or married, and she always felt like she didn't measure up. They were smaller, or taller. She imagined that their husbands or boyfriends were not like hers. Because of this insecurity, she always seemed to feel out of place.

The first time that Rick cheated, she felt like it was her fault. Shelly thought if she had not been such a problem, Rick would be faithful. She was young and innocent and naive. She thought surely if she would have been more of what her husband was looking for, the betrayal would have never happened. If I could speak to Shelly during this vulnerable time, I would tell her how beautiful and perfect she was. I would say, "There is nothing wrong with you. Your youth was stolen. You never had a chance to really find yourself. Even the man you married was perhaps too young and immature to be a husband."

These heartbreaking events and Shelly's insecurities would drive her to a very low place in her life. Because of the lack of knowledge and wisdom of both parties, this downward spiral would carry them further into a life that was full of despair. I can't even begin to fathom the hopelessness that was deep in her young soul.

We see these kinds of emotions a lot in women who have struggled in relationships, marriages, and have been the victim of neglect, abuse, and betrayal. These women become altered versions of their former self, broken. Experts say some people cheat to escape from the pain, from loneliness, in hopes they will find a world where hearts don't break or feel empty. Sometimes the realness of life can push at your soul. It can make you look for relief in other places. Sometimes people find their escape in drugs, shopping, alcohol, and many times, in affairs.

Shelly's husband was irresponsible with everything entrusted to him: her well-being, her love, their stability, their money. No matter how much money came into their home, it was not used wisely. Rick never considered what they may need tomorrow. Shelly often longed to have the finer things in life. She would watch other couples with their new cars, new clothes, newer houses. She would say in her heart, one day I'm going to have those nicer things, then my life will be better. She didn't realize it at the time, but Shelly wasn't actually longing for nicer material things. She envied a happy life, someone to truly love her without conditions. I know as a woman that my greatest desire is to have a solid relationship without fear of despair and loneliness.

When Shelly was 18, her sister kept asking her to come to church. Shelly was raised in church, but she stopped going after her mother passed away. So for six years, likely the years when she needed it most, Shelly wasn't part of a church family. Perhaps it would have offered the security and family she hoped for. Maybe God's love would have been enough so that she wouldn't think she needed Rick's poor excuse of devotion.

The baby was now two years old, and Shelly felt she was learning as she went. She would often tell her son that they grew up together.

This church that her sister attended was an awesome place, but Shelly was apprehensive. She went to please her sister.

Shelly's life would never be the same again. They won her over. It was so renewing, and the love she felt there was nothing like she had ever felt. She was hooked. Eventually, this assembly would be her place of worship, her safe place, a place where the most beautiful love flowed from the most amazing people.

One thing Shelly would notice was how the men treated their wives with respect and honor. Week after week she would leave her husband at home, or wherever he would go, to attend this new-found love. It was God; she knew God was keeping her. The mothers of the church would take her under their wings and love her. They taught her about holiness and modesty. They even taught her about being a wife. She learned that God loved her. This new road she was on wouldn't be an easy road. Her life at home was still difficult. Shelly and Rick separated during the first three years of her going to this church.

With youthful hope and the desire to make a happy home for her little boy, Shelly would go back to Rick because it seemed like the right thing to do. Not long after the reconciliation, Shelly was pregnant again.

Hebrews 10:17
And their sins and iniquities will I remember no more.

Chapter 5: Hoping For Nothing

Things seemed like they improved a bit for a few years. The new baby girl seemed to help ease some of the animosity in the marriage. Perhaps life was settling in or a few years had waned some of the immaturity that compounded many of their issues. Shelly stayed her focus on God, because she knew He was the only secure thing she could hold on to.

Even though the marriage improved and probably seemed fine on the outside, there was a deep unsettling in the air. It was like something was missing. They were intimate; maybe she trusted him a little more now, and they truly had a good physical connection. So why was this loneliness so prevalent? Shelly couldn't get past the chaos that was always right under her facade. Just one wrong word or event could start an avalanche.

From time to time, Rick would hit Shelly across the head or back. No one really knew the physical abuse that went on behind closed doors. And even though it didn't happen as often anymore, on a bad day she still endured a pull to her hair or a slap with an open hand.

Church became Shelly's refuge. She longed to have a relationship like the other couples. In her marriage to Rick, he would often accuse her of having inappropriate relationships with men in her church. It wasn't unusual for her to come home to a chaotic scene. There were times that the interrogating went on all night. Shelly was choked, slapped, and sometimes kicked in her sides. A person can easily be deceived by the Devil into falling from grace, but the consequences at home were never worth letting go of church. It was her place of peace and comfort.

During the last two years of Shelly's marriage to Rick, the love was buried so deep in resentment that somehow she had managed to become numb to her so-called husband. Satan was setting the trap. He knew he was wearing her down. Don't think for a minute that the Devil isn't conniving. The words that kept coming, like wave upon wave, manipulated her state of mind, blurring the edges between right and wrong. "Well, you've been living for God all these years, what have you got to show for it? A sad marriage, all night interrogations. You have nothing." She valued only her two children.

During all their years of marriage, Shelly's husband had left her two or three times for other women. Each time he would return, each time adding to her already failing commitment to him. She was weak. How could she be married yet feel so alone?

It took Shelly a long time to forgive him for the pain and abuse. To this day, Shelly keeps those events buried in her past. It would ruin her life if it could run wild in her mind. Shelly said that it took her many years to find the courage and confidence, but she finally left Rick again and the divorce was final. The divorce shocked many people because of the front Shelly and Rick put on in public.

Years later, even after she remarried, Shelly found herself in a prayer line at a church service. She told her pastor that she truly needed to let go of the feelings that she had toward her first husband. She couldn't even stand to look at him, let alone hear his voice. This anger and resentment was unrelenting in its grip, and she didn't want it to control her. Her pastor spoke into her spirit with words of wisdom. He said anytime you speak of him, speak good things. Try to not speak of the hurt or the bad memories. So Shelly agreed to do this. It wasn't easy. It's still not, so she simply doesn't say anything about Rick most of the time, but she is determined to not let the hurt affect her.

    The hate changes who we are if we let it stay.

Colossians 1:13–14

Who hath delivered us from the power of darkness, and hath translated us into the kingdom of his dear Son:

In whom we have redemption through his blood, even the forgiveness of sins:

Chapter 6: The Trap Is Set

Another couple attended the same assembly where Shelly found refuge: Bill and Suzy. Bill and Suzy were married with children, and their marriage was under attack by the same spirit of infidelity that had made Shelly feel so lonely in her marriage with Rick.

Bill and Shelly met in that church many years ago, and as time passed God began to use them to minister to others. Shelly was a preacher, and so was Bill. Because of the man's position in the church, Shelly found it easy to talk to Bill and trust him. It started so innocently.

A counseling session with Bill began a downward spiral for both of them. Shelly found comfort in his affirmation, something that she never got to feel in her marriage. How could Shelly betray her friend, her sister in the Lord? She knew she should get away from this temptation. Satan had his bait in the right place, and he dangled everything that Shelly longed for in front of her eyes. Satan would tell her, "Shelly, you deserve this kind of love." And she did, but not from Bill, this married man of God.

By the time the affair was in full swing, Shelly was divorced. Going through that divorce made it even easier for Shelly to want to escape into Bill's arms. Bill and Shelly would end up leaving town together, a romantic escapade fleeing God, responsibility, and any moral compass.

Just as we must awake from our dreams in the morning, so did this little trip end quickly. Bill returned home to his wife and children. Shelly knew that was the best decision and was honestly happy he made that choice.

She hoped the damage they had done to the innocent would be repairable, but her life was a total mess. She couldn't go back to her church, the place where she learned to take refuge when her life felt scary and sad. She felt guilty, ashamed, and unworthy.

> *Then drew near unto him all the publicans and sinners for to hear him. And the Pharisees and scribes murmured, saying, This man receiveth sinners, and eateth with them. And he spake this parable unto them, saying, What man of you, having an hundred sheep, if he lose one of them, doth not leave the ninety and nine in the wilderness, and go after that which is lost, until he find it?*
> **Luke 15:1-4**

You know, Satan is the only one that will tempt you, deceive you, cause you to fail, and then condemn you for it.

It seemed like the families of this assembly were under attack by a lustful spirit. Several couples had marital problems. At least two or three of Shelly's good friends were getting divorced. Shelly did not go back to that church. She needed to go on with her life, so she began to go to another church. She hoped to find resolution and forgiveness from God, even if nobody else could offer it. Shelly had one close friend, Beth, that took her under her wing, and she showed Shelly so much grace and mercy. Thank goodness for her!

Beth was like the healing balm of Gilead that is found in Jeremiah 8:22. The healing balm of Gilead was symbolic to Christ. It's a medicinal substance derived from plants. Gilead was a place that was known for its spices and high quality ointment. Beth showed that a true child of God could love so deeply that she would put her own relationships and acceptance at risk to come along beside Shelly in her time of great failure.

She wanted to show Shelly that God loved her and

wanted to forgive her. She would often remind Shelly that Jesus was a friend to sinners. She would spend hours encouraging her to forgive herself and let God be the God He is, merciful.

When people have failed, been disobedient, and hurt others in the process, not many people will stick their necks out for them. Yet Shelly's friend had seen her in her brokenness, even before this awful tragedy had taken place. Because of their close friendship, Beth knew Shelly was trying to fill an emptiness or void with the love she always longed for. She didn't judge her or label her. Beth was the only one Shelly felt she could confide in about her emotional rollercoaster. There have been times in my own life that friends like that were hard to find, so I feel so blessed that God blesses us with friends like that.

We are the hands and feet of Jesus. We are also his mouthpieces. My own failures have turned my heart to be more compassionate and understanding. Not every time that a person fails in adultery is it an honest mistake. Sometimes people will repeat these actions over and over, a behavior, an intentional choice repeated despite the hurt and chaos it causes. The mindset of an individual will play a large part in the moves they make.

I believe Shelly was trying to fill an emptiness but found the mistake left her with a bigger hole until she found the courage and faith to find repair through God. God is and will always be all humans need, but the enemy knows his greatest tactic is to wear us down where we lack the most in our spirits. Let's be thankful for friends that let God rule their hearts and minds and are forgiving and compassionate like Beth.

Isaiah 1:8
And the daughter of Zion is left as a cottage in a vineyard, as a lodge in a garden of cucumbers, as a besieged city.

Chapter 7: Hope Turns

It wasn't easy trying to live that ugly failure down. Shelly kept her distance from everyone because she wanted God to forgive her and help her get back up. She felt convicted. She desired to beg forgiveness from all those she had betrayed, not just Suzy, but to all of the family and friends in the congregation, but a gesture such as this would be like rubbing salt in a wound for both them and for her.

This story is a story of brokenness, failures, guilt, and shame. It's also a story of strength, humility, grace and mercy. After a few months, one of the men from her former church also divorced and began to reach out to Shelly. The damage from Shelly's sin caused her to have a difficult time trusting anybody, yet her loneliness drove her to let this other man into her world. His name was Roger.

After getting to know Roger, Shelly told him that she needed more than just a date. She was a single mom that loved with her whole heart, and she had experienced so much abuse, betrayal, and abandonment that she often felt strapped to an emotional rollercoaster. She needed stability and love, and he either needed to marry her or leave her alone. Well, they married, and he was more than she ever wanted and more. God provided the security and love she needed, despite her feelings of unworthiness, despite her doubt, and despite her big sinful mistake.

The humbling wasn't over yet though. Roger still attended her old church, Bill and Suzy's church. He lived in their community. Roger lived next door to Bill and Suzy, and his landlord was related to Bill. So when Roger and

Shelly got married, Shelly moved in right next door to Bill!

Of course, Suzy had a problem with this. So after several days, the landlord told Roger that he and Shelly had to move. When Roger learned the news and conveyed it to Shelly, she wasn't upset. She knew that seeing Bill continuously and being reminded of her fall would be detrimental to her spirit, and they all recognized it would create conflict in Bill's fragile home. While this consequence of her action played out, God was still in the midst.

> *Flee fornication. Every sin that a man doeth is without the body; but he that committeth fornication sinneth against his own body. What? know ye not that your body is the temple of the Holy Ghost which is in you, which ye have of God, and ye are not your own?*
> **1 Corinthians 6:18–19**

The packing began immediately.

You see friend, sin will take you farther than you want to go and cost you more than you want to pay. Shelly didn't just fail God. She hurt her friends. Her reputation was scarred. It didn't matter what drove her to fall from grace, or even why. It was a sin that would take Shelly years to recover from.

Some people say "sin is sin no matter how big or small," and I agree. But the sin of adultery takes a toll on every aspect of your life. In this case, the consequences even followed Shelly into her new marriage by costing them their home.

"Hope is the thing with feathers that perches in the soul and sings the tune without the words and never stops at all."
–Emily Dickinson

2 Corinthians 5:17–19

Therefore if any man be in Christ, he is a new creature: old things are passed away; behold, all things are become new.

And all things are of God, who hath reconciled us to himself by Jesus Christ, and hath given to us the ministry of reconciliation;

To wit, that God was in Christ, reconciling the world unto himself, not imputing their trespasses unto them; and hath committed unto us the word of reconciliation.

Chapter 8: A Place To Begin Again

So Roger and Shelly moved away from that area to start their new adventure as husband and wife. They went to another church in another town. Things went pretty smooth for the most part and life was moving forward. Shelly's sin was in the rearview.

Roger had always felt the call to pastor, but now that he had a divorce on his record, religious rules in their denomination deemed him disqualified. Roger had these principles drilled into him his entire life. And while I don't intend to dispute anyone's church doctrine or interpretation of the Bible, I hope to show you how two broken people can become whole again.

Two people answered the call of God, let go of all human opinions, and walked out their God given dreams. If it is possible for them, it is possible for you.

But it didn't happen overnight.

Five years passed, and life with Roger was good—he was kind to her and faithful. It was a life that she only dreamed of as a young woman, but there was a pull on Shelly's soul, a longing to go back to her home church. She desperately tried to bury her past, but the past wasn't the problem. Something was missing.

People may have said, "Don't think about home! You've burned that bridge. You have to let it go." That truly would have been easier, if God agreed. Shelly enjoyed the new church, but there was no replacing her home.

"I want to come back home." Those are the words

that rolled out of Shelly's mouth. The voice on the other end of the phone lovingly sighed, "Come on back home then." That voice was such a comforting familiar voice. It was Shelly's former pastor from that church she once called home, the one where she had made the mistake.

Could it be happening?

Could Shelly really be going back?

What happened that made Shelly finally make that call or even want that dramatic move? The church Shelly had recently been attending was of a different organization. The opportunities for her to serve God in an impactful way were much more limited there. They loved Shelly and made her feel welcome, but that longing to walk in her calling was buried deep in Shelly's heart, so deep that she almost forgot what it was like to feel that amazing feeling that comes with being used by God.

Then one day something happened that made her know she had to bury her pride and make that call. She now realized that God had allowed this hurtful situation to occur because He had some work to do in other people's lives from Shelly's former church.

Why would Shelly want to go back to that church? Why couldn't she just find another assembly that would use her in their pulpit? Maybe she could, but truly all Shelly wanted to do was go back home. She was searching for that safe secure place she knew it to be. That place where love filled the air and hearts got comforted.

That following Wednesday night Shelly walked back into her home church. The atmosphere was electric. Emotions were bouncing for everyone. No doubt some were appalled, some nervous, and others were overjoyed.

She knew God was showing her mercy.

Roger didn't accompany her for several weeks. He

> *I will arise and go to my father, and will say unto him, Father, I have sinned against heaven, and before thee, And am no more worthy to be called thy son: make me as one of thy hired servants. And he arose, and came to his father. But when he was yet a great way off, his father saw him, and had compassion, and ran, and fell on his neck, and kissed him. And the son said unto him, Father, I have sinned against heaven, and in thy sight, and am no more worthy to be called thy son. But the father said to his servants, Bring forth the best robe, and put it on him; and put a ring on his hand, and shoes on his feet: And bring hither the fatted calf, and kill it; and let us eat, and be merry: For this my son was dead, and is alive again; he was lost, and is found. And they began to be merry.*
> **Luke 15:18–24**

had not rejected God during these five years away, but he did stumble off his path of closeness and purpose to Him. He attended church with Shelly at the other church, but he didn't claim to live a holy life.

Now faced with Shelly's pleas for him to join her, Roger told her it was embarrassing to him. This church was also Roger's former church as well. When he attended there, he had been married to his first wife. He had been a minister in this church for a few years, but his wife left him and his life had spun out of control shortly after. So to come back divorced and remarried was somewhat humiliating.

Roger had been told his entire life that divorce and remarriage was against God's will. No matter what others told him, Shelly and Roger still believed God would bring things full circle. Soon Roger also couldn't deny the undeniable pulling in his heart to go back home, and it wasn't long before Roger was sitting beside Shelly at their former church.

Roger came back to God. This would start a whole

new journey for both of them. Roger and Shelly both had thrown off all restraints, living like there was no tomorrow. No payday was coming for the ungodly seeds they had sown before`. Just because they had freedom to live as they chose, it didn't come without penance. They realized that God was waiting on them with open arms and better life in store. Just like the prodigal son, they had to go back the way they came to truly realize the magnitude of this restoration process that God was bringing into view.

Could God in all his sovereignty be reaching for them, like a father trying to save a drowning child? Could the God of the universe want two broken people that smell like the pig pen? Yes, he wanted them. His purpose for them was so much more than they could even fathom.

Right in the middle of Roger and Shelly's story, God was reaching for them; and God is reaching for you as well. The father in the story of the prodigal son was watching for his son to return. This is the same as the God of our souls, waiting on us to come back home.

"Sometimes the hardest part isn't letting go but rather learning to start over."
–Nicole Sobon (program 13), The Emile Reed Chronicles

Ephesians 4:31–32

Let all bitterness, and wrath, and anger, and clamour, and evil speaking, be put away from you, with all malice:

And be ye kind one to another, tender-hearted, forgiving one another, even as God for Christ's sake hath forgiven you.

Chapter 9: When Home Feels Unfamiliar

Shelly felt amazing to be home. She was not welcomed by all, especially Bill's wife and family. Somehow Shelly knew that God was working on her behalf. God would bring complete repair before their eyes. Roger and Shelly were slowly proving themselves. They were asked to preach again. Shelly was a singer, and the pastor loved for her to sing. The pastor grew to appreciate and enjoy their new presence. God will always right the wrongs and recompense the outcast.

Suzy came to Shelly after a few months. She wanted to somehow get through this with God's help. She told Shelly, "I need you to help me get over you."

Shelly was shocked yet not surprised. She knew God was orchestrating healing. She responded with mercy and with assurance that she was only there to get back to her place with God. They received the breakthrough they both needed.

Forgiveness is one of God's greatest attributes. When people have been hurt, wounded, or had their trust broken forgiveness takes on a new mask of challenges. We can honestly forgive our offenders. The action of hurt may still linger in the background. God is the only one who can truly give you that kind of strength to forgive. He is the only one that can bring true healing to a devastating event. Shelly was the offender, and she needed God's forgiveness.

God was orchestrating provision, as well. A house became available not long after Roger and Shelly returned to their home church. It actually belonged to their pastor.

> *"Then came Peter to him, and said, Lord, how oft shall my brother sin against me, and I forgive him? till seven times? Jesus saith unto him, I say not unto thee, Until seven times: but, Until seventy times seven."*
> **Matthew 18:21–22**

Shelly knew God was moving on their behalf. You know God is working when certain events are taking place that are pointing toward a restoration. Shelly had yearned in her heart to go back home. God was going above and beyond anything that Shelly could have imagined. Humbled by God's provision, she wanted to share this beautiful redemptive story of grace and mercy.

There was such a strong need of healing in the whole community. Shelly wasn't surprised that some peopled asked forgiveness from her. She knew from her past hurt and wounds she received from Rick that bitterness and unforgiveness can take residence in your heart.

When God is behind the scenes, get ready for some mouth-dropping events to take place. Remember how Roger and Shelly were told to move? This is how God brings things full circle. The pastor had moved out of his old home place. Roger asked if they could move into the empty house. It was probably not the easiest decision, but amazingly the answer was yes. You see my friends, God doesn't have a respect of persons, and neither can we.

They had to wait a few weeks before the house was ready. Shelly couldn't believe it was happening. Not only was God bringing them back to that area, He was moving them into the pastor's old house. At the time, Shelly wasn't thinking about this being a God thing, she just knew that her heart longed to go back home and God was going beyond anything they could comprehend.

Bill and his wife no longer lived down the same

road. They had moved about a mile up the road. It was an exciting time for Roger and Shelly. They were moving out of a very small house into a four-bedroom house. Even though the place had been there for quite a few years, it was nice. It had been remodeled. The house would become a piece of their heart for nine years.

Several people blamed Shelly for her mistake. It was no secret. Shelly understood. Bill's family held her at a distance. They viewed Bill as the victim of temptation and viewed Shelly's presence as a threat to his well-being, happiness, and home.

Shelly didn't deny that she allowed the enemy to use her. Maybe this is one of the reasons I wanted to write this book, for all the Shellys out there. I'm not trying to throw stones. The affair took a toll on Bill's whole family. They were hurt, and the blame was mostly put on Shelly.

It's not fair that only one person gets the blame when affairs take place, though. I can tell you from this story to many others, I know it is true, the woman usually gets the blame. The old saying, "it takes two to tango" may be cliché, but in general, it is true.

There is a story nestled in the book of Judges, a story of a man and woman. You may know them by Samson and Delilah. The story is often referenced when an affair is brought to light. The woman is usually compared to Delilah because she was able to convince this strong man to tell all his heart and let down his guard. This one-sided account seems to kind of sum it up, unless you see the situation from the woman's perspective, the woman being compared to Delilah.

Let's look a little closer. Samson's mother was given specific instructions about the birth of her child. Samson was a Nazarite, and by their law he was not to consume any wine nor strong drink. The mother was told not to eat anything from the vine or to drink wine either. Whatever she consumed would be in his blood. I challenge you to read the story of Samson starting in the book of Judges in the thirteenth chapter. He was not to touch any unclean thing, nor have a razor put to his hair. In these chapters, you find Samson defying every law that was expected of him.

He used the jawbone of an ass to defeat a thousand Philistines. He drank water from the same jawbone. He ate honey from the lion's carcass. He slept with harlots. The only thing left untouched was his hair. Samson was already on his way down, he had all but destroyed his own lineage.

The enemy saw an already weakened man, and of course by Samson's lifestyle they knew he had a weakness for women. They used his weakness and went for the throat. He laid his head in the lap of his own lust one time too many.

The story continues to tell how Samson's enemies offered Delilah a reward for the truth of Samson's strength. Sure, he played a few tricks on her to hide his secret, but just like anything you do wrong, it will eventually catch up with you as it did Samson. The truth of the story is Samson was already weak when the greatest temptation he would ever face came to him through someone he loved.

Unlike King David, Samson didn't get the girl. He also died because of his folly. Let's be fair, when we are on the outside looking in, not every story is the same. But I can tell you when good people fall in this sin, there have usually been a number of events leading up to this fall. And even if Delilah seemed to be the evil tempting serpent, Samson had the right to choose, and he had started relenting to sin and temptation even before Delilah came along.

Somewhere, they touched the forbidden fruit.

They drank from the vine of loneliness or ate from broken dreams. We never know how close a person is to sliding off the edge of the cliff.

One of the days that Shelly and Bill were gone together, Bill went back home for a day to see his children. After he returned, Bill handed her an envelope. It was addressed to her. Her heart was beating hard as she opened the envelope. There was a card with a picture of a big smile, with these words under it, "You finally got what you wanted."

Shelly was furious. She put the card back in the envelope without even opening it and threw it away. To this day, Shelly has no idea who the card was from or what was written inside. She knew that she was being blamed for the whole thing. Oh, the ugliness this fall from grace had cost Shelly. Bill went back home while Shelly was left out in the cold to fend for herself.

Some would say that Shelly deserved every difficulty she encountered after that. Every morsel of gossip about her, every month that she struggled to pay her bills, every minute of regret and loneliness. She was a homewrecker, after all! Right? Bill should be at home, consoling the wife, getting "back to normal" and forgetting all about Shelly.

You see the cycle. The woman gets the blame. The man returned home and all seemed restored. Shelly had no home or family to go back to. Bill was accepted, and Shelly got the boot.

Now, God has beautifully mended the broken and restored the fallen. The raw footage of sin and shame is hard to look at and hard to recover from. It always pays its debt. Only God can redeem in a way that is whole.

The truth is that both had relented to temptation. Both had sinned. And if either of them should be allowed forgiveness, redemption, and repair, shouldn't they both?

Mark 11:25-26

And when ye stand praying, forgive, if ye have ought against any: that your Father also which is in heaven may forgive you your trespasses.

But if ye do not forgive, neither will your Father which is in heaven forgive your trespasses.

Chapter 10: When Healing Is In The Air

Each year brought more and more healing. The neighboring churches that knew about the affair were blown away. What a story of redemption! They watched as Shelly submitted herself to the church. Shelly had been a great asset to the assembly before her mistake. She was going to prove herself again to God and the people.

The community that they moved back to was full of families that were impacted by the mistake. All Shelly could think was, "Wow, God what are you doing?" even though healing had taken place. Mercy had been shown in the place of judgment. Shelly knew God was righting the wrong for both involved. She had no hidden animosity. The scar was there for her to bear, but inside she was whole and stronger.

This wasn't just about Bill and Shelly, this was God recompensing the wrongs on both sides. Sometimes when these acts take place in the confines of the church, there are more hearts that need mending other than the two offenders. And perhaps God used this to set an example, for both others in the church and in the community, that forgiveness and repair is possible even when it seems implausible.

When you think the story can't possibly get more bizarre, it does. Bill and Suzy had moved up the road away from the little community, the same area where Shelly and Roger were asked to move from. Well, Bill and his wife moved back to that area almost right across the road from Shelly and her husband Roger. Even though healing had taken place and mercy had been shown in place of judgment, this was still a situation that was extremely intense. They often ended up outside at the same time. Small talk was the norm between the two couples. Shelly knew that God was righting the wrong.

It was clear that God was showing out. Shelly could honestly say that she had no hidden animosity. She knew that her failure was a scar that she would bear. She had no revenge in her spirit. Even though she may have gotten the raw end of the deal, she was just so humbled by the evidence of God's hand bringing the process to a complete circle. This wasn't about Bill and the fall with Shelly, this was God righting the wrong of how the affair was handled.

The story in Genesis 25 about Jacob swindling his brother, Esau, out of his birthright is a great example of God bringing a situation to climax. The Bible tells us that Jacob and Esau were born twins, Esau first with Jacob holding his heel. They were at odds even in the womb. One day, Jacob convinces Esau to sell him the birthright for a bowl of lentils.

Jacob spends years away from his homeland. Then one day the Lord tells Jacob to go back home. Now Jacob had watched God work on his behalf many times with his father-in-law. To go back home and face the music was a whole different story, or so he thought. You would think that Jacob would not have thought twice about his order to go back home. But he knew the schemes that he played a role in. Jacob was grown and could have simply said no. That's why I believe Jacob was so leery of returning back to his homeland. He knew his heart.

Truth be known, he wanted that birthright as much as his mother wanted him to have it. When their mother,

Rebekah, was carrying the twins she asked the Lord why there was such a struggle between the babies. The Lord told her that she had two nations in her womb, and the elder would serve the younger. God prophesied right there about this very event that would come into play in the years to come.

The story of Jacob tricking Esau out of his birthright was simply prophecy being fulfilled. Nevertheless, Jacob wasn't in a hurry to go see what had become of his brother.

God was also working His plans. I believe these kinds of stories are found throughout the Bible as examples for us. God is a just God. He makes amends. Jacob went back home. Esau forgave him. A new life began for Jacob. I can relate to Jacob though. Sometimes life feels like a big mess, but God comes through for us if we follow His lead.

I believe that just because you have had a moment of sin that causes chaos and disruption doesn't mean that you can't be redeemed in a way that will still allow you to pursue your calling or purpose in life. I speak from what I've experienced in my own walk with God. I along with my husband have our ugly past that the enemy would love to use to break us down and keep us oppressed. We have chosen to move forward at the beckoning pull that is in our hearts. We only know that God has reached down His mighty hand to put us on a path that we could have never followed on our own. My word to you, or someone you may know that has fallen prey to this condemnation, is God did not come to condemn but to save the lost and forgive the fallen.

> *For God sent not his Son into the world to condemn the world; but that the world through him might be saved.*
> **John 3:17**

Go with me on our journey to New Beginnings. Put yourself in our place. Allow yourself to dream again. Pursue those gifts and callings. Envision yourself walking out those dreams. Let God be God and not man. Only you know what you feel and what God is calling you to do. Only you can fulfill those longings that are buried deep inside your thirsty soul.

Let the river of living water quench that parched life. It's like a breath of fresh air blowing over your troubled mind, telling you to get up, get back in the race. Shed those extra weights of shame and guilt. Put on the garment of praise. Run this race with joy and peace.

Part 2: A Different Set Of Eyes

The name of this section, A Different Set of Eyes, sums up the next five views: The Betrayer (the husband), The Betrayed (the wife), the Samaritan woman at the well, the woman caught in the very act of adultery, and the story of Tamar.

The four Gospels of the New Testament is one of the greatest examples of perspective written in God's holy Word. Matthew, Mark, Luke and John all tell the story of specific events about Jesus Christ. We all know each one saw things from a different perspective.

The next five accounts are fictional retellings of perspectives of those involved in a sin that has taken it's toll on many of us. What sin? Adultery. Great liberty was taken with the writing. My views are my own, and these accounts do not intend to assume any thoughts or feelings of other parties. These accounts do not intend stand as fact but as a creative take that offers perspective.

The Betrayer

"Oh, if I could only go back…"
A hundred times over those words rolled off my tongue.
What was I thinking? I knew I should have kept my distance from her. I should have been strong in the midst of her weakness. When I should have been leading her in godly wisdom, I allowed temptation to lead us both astray.
For what I did, my life is forever scarred. I have poured my regrets out before the Lord. I've asked for forgiveness from my children, my wife, my church, and yes, even the woman I cheated with. We really don't realize how vulnerable we are until one of our greatest temptations stands before our eyes.

When she first started coming to church services, she was broken in her spirit. She had small but noticeable bruises on her open skin. It didn't take a rocket scientist to see she'd had a hard life. When our fling started, my intentions and hers were not the same. She was recently divorced, looking for her happily ever after. She needed a man to support and strengthen her. That is why my shame, after it all played out, was almost unbearable at times.

It was a natural high. I don't know what it's like to do drugs, but the feeling I had in those moments, even before we acted on the temptation, was addictive. When life is stressful, we often look for a place to escape to, a place where reality is altered or distant. We look for a place where lack of money, lack of intimacy, even lack of purpose becomes insignificant. Even so, I knew there would be a cost as I was sucked into the deep hole of adultery.

It's difficult to think logically when we're at a low point and temptation beckons us with that escape. Perhaps we don't want to think at all. I started to avoid all those in authority in my ministry. I knew my elders knew something was wrong. They just couldn't put their finger on the problem. It was like I lived for the next fix, the next meeting where she would confide in me, trusting me to help her find resolve in God. As I saw her brokenness in those days, I was disgusted at the man who would destroy a lady as special and fragile as her.

But it wasn't my place.

It wasn't my place to save her. It wasn't my place to sweep her off her feet. It wasn't my place when she was married, and it wasn't my place after God gave me a family of my own and a responsibility to be a leader and pillar in our church.

There is always a fight between good and evil, and when at a place of weakness, stay guarded, especially when doing work for the Lord. Satan can strike even within the walls of the church if we allow him in.

When the adultery finally happened, it was a devastating act of disobedience. It would take a lot of years to get back up from that fall. The shame and guilt, along with humiliation, almost buried me. I put my wife and children in an awful predicament. My finances were dwindling to an embarrassing low. I fought with my wife almost every day. I was surprised she chose to stay with me after what I did, but my wife is stronger than I could ever be.

How could I be such a mess inside the walls of my home and think I could be a man that would lead in God's

Word and work inside the walls of the church?

I was playing two different roles during the time of the mistake. I couldn't be both of those men. It was tearing me apart. I had to make a choice of what kind of man I would be, and I chose wrong back then. I thought it would be easy to leave all the stress behind. I thought I could start over. I thought I could escape.

But like any other high, I had to come down. I had gone too far. What was I thinking? When you fight certain demons, especially those lustful ones, you cannot give place to the devil. You know the old saying, "Give him an inch and he will take a mile;" I say, "Give him your mind for just a few hours and he can take years off your life."

I hope you can learn from my mistakes. It doesn't matter who you are, or where you come from, or even your status quo; we are all at risk of falling into this trap. The enemy will study you. He will watch how you handle situations. He is waiting for the right moment, the moment when you're at your lowest, frustrated with how life is going. The devil knows when to strike because he's the one throwing curveballs at you. I ended up way worse off than I was before. But if you are in that same place now, I can tell you there is still hope.

The woman I cheated with did not stay broken despite what we did. She came back to our church remarried, and I had no doubt that God was behind it. But I feared it wasn't going to be easy to welcome her back, and it wasn't. People had a problem with it at first. Unresolved issues, unforgiveness, and bitterness had taken root in all of us.

The people of the church, my wife, and the kids had all forgiven me, but that was easier to do with the woman gone. Now that she was back, I had to trust that

God would heal the wounds that were left. But I admit, I was skeptical. It definitely wasn't easy.

It was hard to see everybody dealing with the obvious emotions. I realized that maybe I hadn't truly forgiven myself. I kept thinking I should have helped her instead of adding to her already broken life. Life had dealt her a bad hand. I wanted to help, but I only made a mess.

It took the next few years, but God brought us all healing and restoration that I honestly didn't know was possible.

It wasn't easy being in services with her again. All eyes were on our families. People would whisper about us, and they all wanted to know how it would end up. This woman was brave and humble to come back here knowing that she would be under the gun, especially because she was sometimes called on to preach or sing. It goes without saying that those activities were a sore spot. It was more difficult, especially for my wife, when this lady was the center of attention.

I can't express how much strength God was giving all of us, even in the midst of some tough places.

There were days during the process that my wife and I would have some pretty heated discussions, especially when she thought I was being "too friendly" with the woman and she felt reminded of the sin. I knew that my friendship with the woman was forever tainted, but I still wanted to be nice to her. I had to keep my guard up at all times, not for fear of doing wrong, but to be sure to not evoke mistrust or renew hurt feelings.

It was amazing to watch God bring healing to everyone involved. God restored friendship and peace between my wife and this woman. I'd even go so far as to say they have trust and true sisterly love.

God let my mistake be brought back before me so I could find complete repair. Not only did I have to ask both women for forgiveness, but beyond my words I have tried with all my heart and soul to prove myself to my wife, my God, my church family, and also to the woman I cheated with, that I'm sorry for letting down my blood-stained banner, for not being a true friend when she really needed guidance.

We've both made reconciliation with God. I feel like she paid her dues. God has given her a wonderful man of God. God is restoring double for the shame. My deepest desire is that God will continue to restore, rebuild, reestablish so that this situation can be an example to others who think there is no hope after they have fallen.

God has truly been an anchor through all this journey. My shame still lurks at the corners of my mind, but I know that I am blessed in the end. God allowed me to keep my family, my friends, my church, and continue my calling after I put it all at risk. One thing is for sure, though, I will forever give God the praise for the mending, healing, and restoration.

The Betrayed

I thought she was my friend. But what kind of woman would stoop so low as to take advantage of her friend's husband?

She was always trying to be a part of our relationship. She knew we were having problems. We struggled like most couples. As things were getting more difficult, there was a part of me that didn't even want to be around him. Without a doubt, my so-called friend picked up on that. Yet, he was still mine.

We marry in the church thinking that the one we choose will always be faithful and true. This is definitely a misconception. I wish I had known that simply existing in the church together didn't secure our safety or protect us from strife and temptation. The Bible says in Romans, "all have sinned and come short of the glory of God."

Who thinks at the time of marital problems that there could possibly be another woman? I certainly could not have imagined what the next few months and years were going to bring to my already broken spirit.

I knew something was wrong with my husband, something more than our internal problems. Things made more sense when the truth was revealed. The distance in our marriage got even wider, and the words that were spoken cut deeper each time.

He tried to justify cheating on me. There's nothing that can prepare even someone strong in the Lord for the pain of cheating. Yes, I'm a Christian, but I certainly wasn't prepared for dealing with my husband having an affair with one of my closest friends.

I know I had a right to leave my husband. Adultery is a biblically sound reason to leave a marriage, and after all the problems we were having before, I won't say I didn't consider it. I felt so alone in these times. But my children depended on me to be a good mom and to hold myself together. I wanted to hold myself together for my own sake, too. My marriage and our church were my whole world, and I didn't want to give it all up because of a mistake.

> *And one shall say unto him, What are these wounds in thine hands? Then he shall answer, Those with which I was wounded in the house of my friends.*
> **Zechariah 13:6**

But you better believe I was mad! I was hurt. No, not hurt. I was crushed. This was a double whammy. Betrayed by my husband and stabbed in the back by a sister that I thought had my back. She certainly was on my list of the lowest of low.

But surprisingly, I don't feel that way today. I can honestly say that I have forgiven her and my husband. Some days are harder than others. The wound is still there. Forgiveness on this level doesn't happen overnight. But healing is happening.

I was shocked and appalled when she returned to our church. My heart wasn't ready for it, and everyone in the church, including me, was wondering how it was going to play out.

My husband and I had worked hard to repair our

marriage and move on, and here she was threatening everything we'd rebuilt. I try not to dwell on the hurtful past, and there was a part of me that hoped it would work out for the best, but not tearing her apart in those days was the hardest thing I've ever done. Still, I'll admit, she was brave to come back.

She kept her distance at first. She was not the same as I remembered. In fact, her focus seemed to be solely on getting closer to God. I started to realize, slowly, that she wasn't here to stir up strife or focus on me and my husband. I saw her regret. She seemed determined to prove herself to God and everyone else. It was honestly infuriating at first, but I knew God was working in the midst of it all.

My spirit struggled with unforgiveness, bitterness, and resentment, but slowly, surely, God led me to a new understanding. He was showing me what true forgiveness means. He was showing me how, despite anything human beings do, we have His ultimate love and forgiveness, and I had to forgive her too. Just "moving on" and burying the past was not going to be enough. I needed to allow God to provide full restoration.

But how?

Believe me, it was a grueling process. Some nights I didn't even want to go to church. My conversation with God would go something like this, "Lord, this is hard. How do I worship when my mind is so full of negativity? My mind is clouded by the past, but I want to receive of you."

Over time, the struggle began to ease. The woman remarried, and the more I could see she and her husband were growing in God, the safer I felt. The first time I shook her hand and looked her in the eye, I felt the bonds of unforgiveness loosen. I saw her sincerity, that she was really here for good and not evil.

We still kept our distance, even though we might shake hands and exchange pleasantries, the closeness wasn't there anymore. When she got up to preach or sing, I squirmed. The tension seemed like it was always there. I didn't want to be close to her after what she had done, but little by little, I found that I could tolerate her. Then, little by little, with God's help, I started to find true forgiveness for her. I saw her going after God, and I wanted to please my Savior as well. I'm only human, I know. But I'm also a child of God.

Through His grace, my feelings began to change. I started to see her side. When the offense happened, this woman had been at a weak point. Did I excuse her? No. Did I excuse my husband? No. But gaining understanding loosened more bonds within me. Life is not always pretty or easy. Festering in my anger and distrust was allowing this thing to continue to hurt me.

I had to give it to God. I had to give it to God every day. I had to give it to God every time I saw her for a while. I had to give it to God if I had any hope of ridding myself from the shadow this sin was casting on me.

I sought God many times for His unwavering love that I needed so desperately. Over time, God began to answer. God always knows how to bring us to that exact place that we need to be to surrendered to all His good things. The woman would occasionally remind me of her remorse. My heart knew that she truly wanted to make sure that I felt secure, but her remorse couldn't make it one hundred percent right.

Then one day, God moved. We were at our home church. I saw her through new eyes, and the Holy Spirit stirred within me. My heart was beating so loud in my ears. God was speaking to me, "go get her and go to the altar for prayer." I did. I was happy to. I wanted things to be right between us again.

> *"Can two walk together, except they be agreed?"*
> **Amos 3:3**

The ministers prayed over us. You could feel the power of reconciliation in the service. People gathered around us with great love and compassion for our relationship.

That night, something shifted in my spirit. A closeness began to form between us again. God allowed me to see her brokenness in a new way, to see a woman that truly wanted to make things right. She was only human too. She was someone who loved our family with a godly love.

Some people may feel like she will never be the person that God intended her to be. She and I feel differently. Failure isn't final. Life is not over. We both have just begun to live again under the light of God's forgiveness.

The woman and her husband no longer attend our assembly. Did God move them? Without a doubt, He did. But this time it was not because there were problems, but simply because God had done the work He wanted to do in our relationships. Now all involved can freely move forward with no blocks in their way. It is a beautiful story of redemption and humility.

She didn't have to come back; she could have moved on with her life. But I thank God, she yielded to her desire to come back home even when it wasn't the easy thing to do. We never know what is buried in our hearts till we are faced with unresolved hurts. It's been a grueling process yet a needed one.

Watching other marriages suffer from betrayal has made me realize that my heartbreaking incident was not an isolated case. It took me a few years to be able to even try to make sense of all that had happened. Now I can truly say that my prayers are earnest toward her. I want to see her have the best life that she could have.

My heart is fixed. My life is whole in Christ.

My heart goes out to my friend renewed or anyone who has fallen into that trap of the temptation of adultery. I've been able to help other women who have gone through similar battles. Often, it happened in the church, most of the time by their friends or others they knew well.

My life today is not perfect. There have been many difficult days in my short years here on earth. Through it all, I've learned to totally depend on God. Even through the hard times, I can't complain.

A Different Set Of Eyes:

Stories From The Bible

The Appointment For Grace
John 4

Who am I?

My name was not mentioned, yet my story was placed in the greatest book in the world. Why would the Savior even carry on a conversation with me? My past was riddled with acceptance issues. I longed for a relationship that would fulfill me, evident by my multiple marriages. My culture was of unwanted people. Others scoffed at the people here. I was a Samaritan. Each of my five husbands had tried to make a happy home with me. Looking back now, I realize that I didn't even know what I longed for. I tried many times to quench a thirst that no natural man could quench.

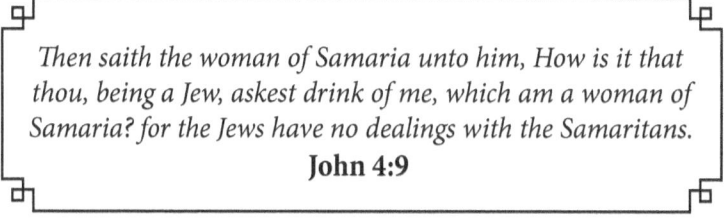

Then saith the woman of Samaria unto him, How is it that thou, being a Jew, askest drink of me, which am a woman of Samaria? for the Jews have no dealings with the Samaritans.
John 4:9

To be honest, it didn't bother me to walk away from one relationship and pursue another. I meant to find satisfaction, whatever that meant. In the time of my era, being divorced and remarried was not necessarily an uncommon event, so maybe it was okay to just keep trying men on like a pair of shoes until I found the one that fit.

I would draw my needed water for daily routines from Jacob's well. This day started out like any other. I got up, gathered what I needed, and headed to the well. But what happened there would change my life and many others. I would become a voice for the Savior.

When I arrived, I saw a Jew sitting by the well.

My mind wondered, "Why is this Jew here? They have no dealings with us Samaritans. Where did He even come from? How did He get here?" So I was admittedly shocked when this Jew spoke to me. He asked me if I would give Him a drink.

He lovingly responded to me in a way that I never could have anticipated. It was like some kind revelation that I was supposed to understand. He offered me a drink that I would never thirst again, yet He had nothing to draw with and nothing in His hand. How could He give me a drink without a vessel?

I had questions. What was this living water? What kind of water was this that He was offering to me? The water in the well would only quench natural thirst. So yes, I wanted this drink. Give me this water that would satisfy every deep longing that I ever had.

Go call your husband, come hither. It was embarrassing. Why did He want me to call my husband? I was not short on having husbands in my past. Plus, why did it matter? Couldn't He just give me the drink? So without making eye contact, my reply was quick. "Sir, I have no husband." He spoke back the words that pierced my soul, a sure sign that this was no ordinary man. "You have spoken the truth, you have had five husbands and the man you're living with now is not your husband." He probably could have put His hand under my chin to close my dropped mouth.

I said, "You must be a prophet to tell me things of this nature. Sir, I know that a Messiah is coming, which is called Christ, when He comes He will tell us all things." I was not prepared to hear His response. My mind was trying to wrap itself around the words that he'd already spoken.

"I that speak unto thee, am He," He replied.

What was happening? What could this encounter mean for me? The Christ, the chosen one was actually carrying on a conversation with me, the Samaritan with a broken past.

There were some followers of Christ that returned to the well, to Jesus. I would find out later as my story was written in the Holy Bible these were His disciples. I was there as they approached Him. You could tell by the looks on their face that they were surprised. Why was He talking to me, a Samaritan woman? It was apparent to them that I was not a respectable lady. What did Jesus want from me?

> *And upon this came his disciples, and marvelled that he talked with the woman: yet no man said, What seekest thou? or, Why talkest thou with her?*
> **John 4:27**

That day my soul got the drink that it so desperately needed. That drink would be a world-changing drink. I dropped my water pot and ran back to the city, proclaiming the Messiah had come. Christ had come to Samaria. I told the people to come see a man that told me all the things I ever did. The people were amazed. They all began to run to the well, to this man who would forever change our destiny.

My life would never be the same again. Even though I was not considered to have the opportunity that was given to me, it was still given. The water of life, Christ, had stepped into my world and given me another chance at life. I would go down in history as the first woman evangelist in the book of John. Many Samaritans that day became believers.

Jesus knew He had an appointment with me.

He'd picked the perfect time, the perfect place. As I read my story, my heart swells from the mercy that was shown to me that day at the well. When I read the part "He must go through Samaria," I see the greatest love that I could have ever encountered was already prepared for me.

The Savior was coming to speak directly to me so I could run with this great message of redemption. You, too, can have this same water. The water of forgiveness. The water of restoration. The water that will cover your past, bring new beginnings to an old situation. Even thousands of years later, my story is still shining light on broken lives. There is life after the mistake.

Yours Truly,
The Samaritan Woman at the Well

The Very Act
John 8

What was happening? My half naked body was being dragged down the street.

"We have caught you, adulteress."

I could hear their statements. It happened so fast my mind couldn't grasp the actions that were taking place. I just knew that the man participating in this same act was fading behind me as they dragged me down the street. There was no way I could get away from them. I was outnumbered. They were men, and I was a woman.

> *And the scribes and Pharisees brought unto him a woman taken in adultery; and when they had set her in the midst, They say unto him, Master, this woman was taken in adultery, in the very act.*
> **John 8:3-4**

It felt like my heart was going to beat out of my chest. There I was, sitting in the presence of Jesus. Where was my lover? Surely they had grabbed him, too. Maybe they were letting him put on clothes. My eyes couldn't look up. My face was burning as I was trying to cover the parts of my body that were so shamefully showing. It wasn't just Jesus, there were other people around him. They brought me into the temple where Jesus was teaching.

Their accusations

> *Now Moses in the law commanded us, that such should be stoned: but what sayest thou? This they said, tempting him, that they might have to accuse him. But Jesus stooped down, and with his finger wrote on the ground, as though he heard them not.*
> **John 8:5-6**

burned in my ears. "We caught her in the very act of adultery. This is an ungodly activity that she participates in often. What will you do about this, Jesus?" They were asking Jesus to make me pay for my wrongs. They had brought their stones with them, because the law stated a person was to be stoned to death for this kind of sin.

 I wondered again about the man I was with, but fear had me silenced. The tension was unbearable. The lump in my throat was causing me to take short breaths. Was this my fate? Was all my sinful life about to unfold before everyone? Was I going to die today? The law said I would. The accusers wanted me dead.

> *And again he stooped down and wrote on the ground. And they which heard it, being convicted by their own conscience, went out one by one, beginning at the eldest, even unto the last: and Jesus was left alone, and the woman standing in the midst. When Jesus had lifted up himself, and saw none but the woman, he said unto her, Woman, where are those thine accusers? hath no man condemned thee? She said, No man, Lord. And Jesus said unto her, Neither do I condemn thee: go, and sin no more.*
> **John 8:8–11**

 Then He bent over, reaching out his hand. Was He about to throw the first stone? But then, Jesus began to write in the sand. It was as if He didn't hear them. While Jesus continued to write on the ground, they continued asking Him, "Jesus! Doesn't the law say, she should be stoned to death?"

 He had to have heard my heart's cry even though I spoke no words as they accused me. I didn't want to die, but I didn't want to live this way anymore. This seemed to be my fate. Nobody had ever reached out to me to tell me life could be different than the one I was living.

Why did I seek comfort in those sinful ways? When I was participating in these shameful acts, my mind never contemplated my wrong-doing. For just that moment in time, I felt fulfilled. Someone needed me, someone was responding to me, even if it wasn't in the right way. There was an empty place in my soul, a place that yearned for real love, a love that felt safe and complete.

Maybe you're there now, or you have been in a place that felt so empty, that to die would be a comfort to you. No woman wants to feel unwanted, unloved, or undesirable. As I read my story in the Holy Bible there was so much behind the scenes that was not revealed that day. My accusers didn't care about my story. They weren't even worried about my failure. It was all about trying to force Jesus to obey the law of Moses. It was about being right and law over love.

Jesus knew their hearts. He knew my heart. It was clear that I was guilty. Everything pointed to my execution. Even now as I see my story in writing, the feelings of gratitude still flood my soul.

Jesus wrote in the sand that day. The Bible does not record what was written by the very finger of our Messiah, but I believe He wrote the sins of those accusers that day for all to see. When He spoke the words, "let he who is without sin cast the first stone," Each person walked away one by one. My life flashed before my eyes. I knew that I was getting a second chance.

Jesus could have stoned me that day, because truly He had committed no sin! Jesus was not trying to impress anyone. He turned to me and simply asked, where were my accusers? Where were the people that condemned me? I replied, there are none. And He said, Neither do I condemn thee, go and sin no more.

My search for love in all the wrong places ended that day. Forgiveness had been granted to me. Jesus showed His unfailing love to me. He showed me His reason for existing. I mattered to Him, which was truly all my soul had ever longed for.

If I could speak into your heart today, I would tell you that Jesus is for you. That you're His number one priority. He wants to be your all and all. He wants to be your reason to get up each day, to face every day with assurance knowing that He loves you more than any mortal could comprehend. My life was forever changed on that shameful day. I will never go back to that lifestyle again. He thought I was worth saving. He went the way of the cross for all of mankind. Not just for the rich, not just for the well to do people, not even just for the good people. But for all. For you. For me.

My name was not mentioned either, but just like the Samaritan woman at the well, you will read our stories in the most read book in the world. To me, that is a sure sign that He knows that we as humans are prone to sin. We have sinful nature. Many stories that have been displayed in the Bible are for a greater purpose. I believe mostly to show how merciful, loving, and forgiving our Savior is.

Yours Truly,
The Adulterous Woman

The Widow's Garment
Genesis 38

I put on that widow's garment like I was told. My father-in-law had all but forgotten me. He promised me his third son when he reached the age of marriage. I was married to his first two sons and the Lord slew them because of their wickedness. Judah's wife died also after a while.

> *Then said Judah to Tamar his daughter in law, Remain a widow at thy father's house, till Shelah my son be grown: for he said, Lest peradventure he die also, as his brethren did. And Tamar went and dwelt in her father's house.*
> **Genesis 38:11**

There I was, doing what I was told to do, but Judah didn't keep his word. The third son was grown and still I wasn't given to him. I know that my story is very hard to read about, and it's probably even hard to imagine someone could do what I did. I meant to make him pay for how I was treated.

It wasn't long until Judah was comforted after losing his wife, and he was back out living his life again. I pondered what I could do to preserve the seed that was rightfully mine. I put aside that widow's garment and put on a new outfit; I disguised myself as a harlot. I knew just where to stand so that he would be tempted to come lay with me.

> *And she put her widow's garments off from her, and covered her with a vail, and wrapped herself, and sat in an open place, which is by the way to Timnath; for she saw that Shelah was grown, and she was not given unto him to wife. When Judah saw her, he thought her to be an harlot; because she had covered her face.*
> **Genesis 38:14–15**

He offered me a baby goat from his flock for pay, and I agreed to lay with him. I knew I would need proof, so I asked for his signet, his bracelets, and his staff. I got what I wanted. I conceived. I laid aside that harlot robe and put back on my widow's garment. If he could play games, so could I.

He sent his friend with the baby goat the next day to pay the harlot he slept with, but she was nowhere to be found. I knew it was just a matter of time before the truth came out. When he heard I was with child and had played the harlot, he wanted me punished, burnt is what he said.

When I stood before him, I stood there with all the items he left with me just three months earlier. He hung his head in shame. He told me I was more righteous than him, because he didn't keep his word about his other son. More righteous is probably not the words you would expect to be called after deceiving your father-in-law to sleep with you.

> *When she was brought forth, she sent to her father in law, saying, By the man, whose these are, am I with child: and she said, Discern, I pray thee, whose are these, the signet, and bracelets, and staff. And Judah acknowledged them, and said, She hath been more righteous than I; because that I gave her not to Shelah my son. And he knew her again no more.*
> **Genesis 38:25–26**

There I stood, pregnant by my father-in-law. Not with just one child but two. They were boys. I named one Zarah and the other Pharez. There was a struggle in my womb, the one that was going to be last broke forth and came out of the womb first.

The old saying "the last shall be first," definitely was in this story. It's true that I played the harlot and got what I thought was rightly mine, seed from that lineage. Back in my day being a mother meant life or death, remembered or forgotten. Before you judge me, just know in the book of Matthew, the first chapter, my son was in the lineage of king David, which runs down to Jesus Christ.

I know it seems like I broke through right in the middle of Joseph's story in the book of Genesis. Sometimes God does the most unlikely thing to prove a point or to make things right. I'm glad he allowed me to be part of this event to bring a more clear picture to the broken, confused, and lost.

God can and will make things right if you only let him have his way in your life. My name is Tamar and what I did will forever be recorded in the Holy Bible.

Yours Truly
Tamar, Mother of Pharez

The Road To New Beginnings

For the gifts and calling of God are without repentance.
Romans 11:29

The Textors step into their God-called purpose in Blytheville, Arkansas. The church they pastor still gathers together in this little red brick building.
Photo by Kendra Leeann Textor

Romans 11:29 is not hard to understand. It doesn't say the gifts are meant only for those who have never failed. In fact most of the Bible is addressed to the Church, God's people. I know I have used King David as an example already, but his story speaks for itself.

Turn, O backsliding children, saith the LORD; for I am married unto you: and I will take you one of a city, and two of a family, and I will bring you to Zion:
Jeremiah 3:14

Here, Jeremiah is married to the backslider.

You see my friend, knowing God's Word helps you with perspective and understanding even in the most difficult situations. One of the most eye-opening scriptures in the Bible for me is found in Hosea 4:6, which says, "my people are destroyed for lack of knowledge."

While not excusing sin, you can still find redemption. I want to convey to you that God is a merciful God. He is very forgiving. We cannot undo our failure, nor make it disappear. But what we can do is receive God's forgiveness and leave the past behind. Let it be a learning experience and not a stumbling block. If you wait on man's approval you may never get back in the race. But God allows you to run a new race.

> *And Jesus said unto him, No man, having put his hand to the plough, and looking back, is fit for the kingdom of God.*
> **Luke 9:62**

Now I don't know how you see this verse, Luke 9:62, but it seems to say that anybody that has fallen or backslidden is not fit for the Kingdom of God. Thank God for forgiveness. No, we are not worthy, but the blood of Christ makes us clean and whole again.

He doesn't want us to sin. He doesn't want us to commit adultery. Sin is sin in the eyes of God. Don't be deceived though, because some acts of sin will have a much larger price on them. There is only one sin that cannot be forgiven. That is blaspheme. That passage of scripture is found in Matthew 12:31.

The act of adultery, affairs, and fornication all fall in the same family of sin. Can it be forgiven? Yes. Be ready for a time of rebuilding trust and reputation. Sometimes it can take years, but it can be done.

> *My little children, these things write I unto you, that ye sin not. And if any man sin, we have an advocate with the Father, Jesus Christ, the righteous.*
> **1 John 2:1**

The Devil does not want us to know biblical truth. He wants you to take the words of people that are not knowledgeable in the Bible. My husband and I are both witnesses of this tragedy. They say you cannot do what God has called you to do if you have been married more than once. I'm not here to dispute beliefs. What I will share with you is how God took both of us and began to call us out of our comfort zone. We had settled in for the long haul. We were minding our own business and trying to forget the past when God began to pull on our hearts.

Getting Free From Being Stuck

I know you have been stuck before. It may have been in a job or maybe a relationship. This is the story about two people that had callings on their lives but felt like they had to let them go because of past sin. You will find in the pages of this journey how we broke free from the mindset of settling for staying stuck. It will reveal to you how life can be all that you dreamed of and more.

The metaphor of a butterfly is one of my favorite examples of transformation. I know how it feels to be boxed in, not only by people or circumstances, but by your own limited thinking.

You know you were made for more. There is a whole world of opportunity to embrace just past your own boundaries. For some reason, though we will continue to go through years of the same routine, I don't believe God wants his people to live just by the hair of their chin. But like the butterfly we will go through a process of transformation to fulfill our true purpose.

What is my purpose? What is my gift? Where does God want to take me? These are questions that I believe we all ask at some point in our lives. For me, I had to spend years in a questionable season. For a three-year period, I was without guidance or words of prophecy. It was not an idle season. In fact, it was quite busy: reaching out, traveling to conferences, having special events. So you might ask how I felt bound? In my spirit. This whole time I was asking, seeking, and knocking; I was trying to find my place and God's purpose for me.

Maybe you are there now. You know that God has spoken to you, but it seems like time is standing still. People all around you are doing great things in the kingdom of God. You may go to different events hoping and praying that you will get some kind of direction for your life. You may see other people receive prophecies. There you are, seemingly getting nothing.

I tell you with all my heart to hold on because your day is coming. Seek Him with all your heart, in time He will surely answer.

Of course it can be lonely and frustrating while God is growing and preparing you. There may be only a few friends that will come along beside you during this season and that's okay. Stay focused on the end results. It will feel uncomfortable at times because it's a time of stretching. Telling you these emotions is not to scare you but to encourage you. When my three-year season ended it was like everywhere I went God allowed someone to speak into my life. Confirmations of many things downloaded in my spirit during this season.

Let me build your faith up with the words of this book, by following our journey to our New Beginnings. If you can relate, you know there is more for you in your walk with God. Don't put this book down. Because only God could have opened this great door for us. He also brought this book forth out of my heart. Can I say without spoiling the end of this story, eyes have not seen, nor ears heard what God has prepared for all of us?

    Passion has met purpose. The journey has truly been a beautiful experience. We will never go back to the humdrum life of mediocrity. So if you're ready to know how God brought my husband and me to this part of New Beginnings, then let's move forward and read on.

Don't Mistake Heaven's Contractions For Demonic Attacks! Birthing Is Painful.

Part 3: New Beginnings

The Textor family smiles on the steps of their church.

Photo by Kendra Leeann Textor

*For I know the thoughts that I think toward you, saith
the Lord, thoughts of peace, and not of evil,
to give you an expected end.*
Jeremiah 29:11

Chapter 1: A New Path

Emotions were high. Excitement was in the air. We rushed up the steps to our new building. Even putting the key in the lock was such a delightful experience. It was our first service, February 11, 2018; we were not even bothered that no one was there but us. We knew God had sent us.

Five years of praying and seeking God for direction had finally paid off. We had been knocking on doors like the Bible tells us to: ask, seek, and knock. My husband spent almost a year looking; he even looked in a different town. I was just trying to be the encourager. I didn't know what God had planned for us. I knew enough of the Bible to know that for God to work effectively we had to be in one accord.

But let's back up a bit.

My life began to take a major turn in 2014. I was never a reader until that year. We were helping my mother-in-law pack up a few things to move. I remember picking up a book to just kind of scan through it because the title jumped out at me. I decided to take a break, sat down, and I began to read the introduction. To my surprise, I couldn't put it down. It was like a light came on in my spirit.

The book was a thirty-day declaration. The name of it was *I Declare,* written by Joel Osteen. It had such an impact on me that I took the book home and read the whole thing within two days.

My life was okay, but I had no idea the work that God was fixing to do in me. He was pulling the cover off of my outlook on life through a book and a decision that would later be one of the most incredible pieces of my life. This book revealed to me where I was, which certainly wasn't pretty. Negative talk and thoughts were ruling me, and I didn't even know it. I was calling defeat into my situation every day.

My words needed to change.

That book sparked a love of reading in me. I started reading more and more. As I read book after book, my knowledge of the Bible began to grow in leaps and bounds. Life had taken on a new meaning. The books opened my heart to pray in ways I had never prayed. A sleeping giant had awoken. Dreams and callings were knocking at my heart. Each new book I read would add coals to a kindling fire. The passion began to burn in my soul. Visions of me speaking at events began to show up in my spirit.

Sometimes I would wake up in the middle of the night or early in the morning, often 2 or 3 a.m. These awakenings came with revelation from God, and they were coming more and more often. My prayer life went to a whole new level. Writing down prayers. Writing out scriptures and declaring his promises over my life.

"Why now?" was my question. Why was this shaking my life like never before? It was very exciting watching God do a work in me and to hear from God in the night hours.

Everyone could see the change. They could feel the change. There was an undercurrent in the atmosphere. The books that I was reading were teaching me how to pray effectively. Just pushing through my little prayer time was a thing of the past.

Books like *Change Your Words, Change Your Life* by Joyce Meyers, and other authors like Charles Swindoll and Max Lucado were changing my whole world and I loved it.

My preaching took to a new level. Other churches began to ask me to come and speak at their events. Overjoyed could not describe how I felt about the change that was happening in me and my life. Now more than ever I felt the need to find my purpose.

Behold, I will do a new thing; now it shall spring forth; shall ye not know it? I will even make a way in the wilderness, and rivers in the desert.
Isaiah 43:19

Chapter 2: The Job Had To Go

All this change also began to shift the way I looked at my job. I felt discontent. Why the sudden distaste in my spirit for a job that I had worked at for almost eleven years? Before 2014 was over, I quit my job as a deli manager.

All this had stemmed from picking up one book that read my mail. It made me want more from life. It was truly a pinnacle point for my destiny. The income from my job was a great deal of our money source. My husband never really said a lot about my decision to quit. We definitely felt the loss in our finances.

Many times in my prayer closet, the battle would get bloody, but I knew I had heard from God about leaving that job.

"You won't always be here." These are the words that reverberated in my spirit around 4 a.m. on a morning in January 2015. Startled by the realness of the moment, I asked God, what do you mean? From this house? From my home church of thirty something years? How long? The questions just rolled out without me even thinking too much.

"Time, times and a half," was the answer.

Like Mary when the angel told her she would conceive, that the Holy Ghost would overshadow her, I pondered these sayings that I heard.

A few weeks went by before I shared this word with my husband. I knew the quote was from the Bible, but I wasn't quite sure what it meant. Of course, he knew exactly the meaning, three and a half years. So this was a big thing for us.

We immediately adjusted our prayer life and our fasting. It was exciting yet scary.

Weeks turned into months, then a year passed with little change. Our faith was being tested through my decision of leaving my job. The rich peace and knowledge that we were gaining through this process was priceless. I was changing, and going back was not an option.

I poured myself into the church. My free time was spent investing in my walk with God. I spent time in prayer for several hours a day; I encouraged people through text and social media messenger. I wanted to be used by God any way I could be used. Ideas were flooding my mind. Evangelism, ladies' gatherings, renting space to have seminars. My spirit was reaching and searching for purpose. Seeking fulfilment was at the top of my list.

Being away from my job gave my mind more time to pursue the calling. During one of the early mornings of God speaking to me, He told me He was giving me back the years that the cankerworm stole from me. Again, I was left to ponder on that. Looking up the word *cankerworm* really gave me the extra push I needed. The cankerworm can apparently destroy a whole orchard if it's not caught in a short time!

My youth had been stolen from me. Callings and dreams had laid dormant for many years; I wasn't even aware of some of them. My childhood was fraught with neglect and hurt.

Without a job consuming my time, I was able to go to conferences, retreats, and church camps. In 2016, I ventured out and flew for the first time to Miami, Florida for the Women Ministering to Women Conference, and it was even better than I could have hoped.

This little Arkansas girl was learning how to dream. Nothing was lost or in vain, though many times it seemed as though nothing prevailed. Still lingering in the back of our minds were the words about us not always "being there."

I was invited to speak at a prayer conference in Memphis, Tennessee in June 2017. Of course, I accepted. The services were awesome. While at this meeting, I was invited to come preach a three night revival in Memphis.

My heart's desire was truly to give a life changing message (or at least be a blessing). I prayed and sought God for a word from Him to give this assembly. It was located in a rough neighborhood, but my faith was strong. Determined to give it my best, I went each night and preached with purpose and passion.

The little building and congregation were a challenge for my spirit. Nobody knew what was running through my mind. "Just take me to the muddy Jordan and drown me." It didn't take long for God to admonish me. I repented quickly, and the word of God came forth with a powerful anointing. It was a small crowd, only about twenty-five people, but I preached like there were more than a hundred people.

For who hath despised the day of small things?
Zechariah 4:10

Despise not small things. Small things lead to greater things, which lead to new beginnings.

Ask, and it shall be given you; seek, and ye shall find; knock, and it shall be opened unto you:
Matthew 7:7

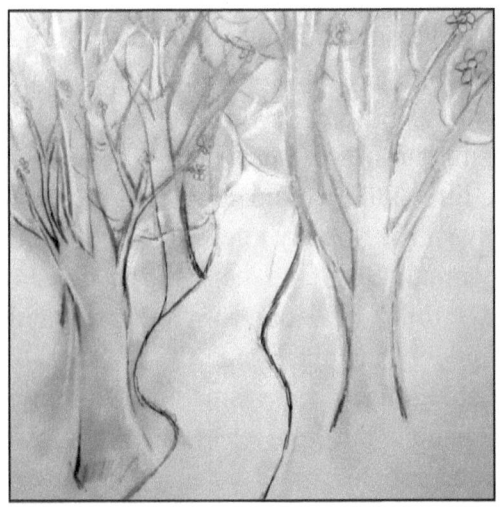

Chapter 3: Knocking On Doors

I spent 2016 and 2017 seeking a specific direction. They were defining years. During this time, my husband was fasting as many as seven days without food, only water. Saturday and Sunday were being used to search for buildings or anything that God may want to use us in. Talk about being radical, passionate, and driven! My husband was relentless on finding the open door. He would stand on the corner of main intersections in some nearby cities wearing some homemade signs that had writing on the front and back. The writing consisted of offering prayer to anyone that needed it. It also was offering them Jesus as their answer to their life's problems.

We had to be on the same page, even when we didn't see eye to eye. The Bible tells me, "how can two walk together unless they agree?" God is not the author of confusion. So many days I just stayed quiet. There was an undercurrent moving in our lives and we knew that something was coming.

The words that God spoke into my spirit were, "There is a place by me." I spent a lot of my morning prayer times seeking God's direction. One particular morning, my spirit seemed confined, I couldn't move forward. My heart was heavy and my mind was so full of desires.

I needed to hear from God.

Where is my place? was the question that weighed heavily in my spirit.

It seemed like everyone was getting to do what God called them to do. People were traveling to preach. People

> *And the LORD said, there is a place by me, and thou shalt stand upon a rock.*
> **Exodus 33:21**

were being promoted within the church. In a way, I was jealous. I was having a pity party for myself. How loving our heavenly Father is though, to speak even in our uncertainty. This saying is found in Exodus 33:21.

The Lord instructs Moses to go forward unto the land that He has sworn to give them. He is telling Moses that the people are stiff-necked and rebellious. If you read the whole chapter you will see God is angry at them, yet He is still wanting to take them forward. Moses is asking God to show him the next step. He wants to know what is in the future for him and the people.

In order for God to show Moses his future, He had to hide him in a cleft of the rock. This passage lets me know that God has got me. I'm covered by His hand of protection. He already has my path laid out for me. I can move forward without fear or doubt. Because He said I have a place by Him. I'm

> *And the LORD said unto Moses, I will do this thing also that thou hast spoken: for thou hast found grace in my sight, and I know thee by name.*
> **Exodus 33:17**

planted on the rock, which is Christ. It didn't matter what others were saying or doing because He had me right where He wanted me. What a consolation knowing that He has us covered. We truly have a God that wants us to succeed in our purpose.

God told me we wouldn't always be where we were at the beginning of 2015. Until the end of 2018, the space of three years, I heard only from God. I did not receive any prophetic words or major visions. People on social media were telling how someone spoke prophecy and light into their life. I witnessed great and marvelous things happening at different church functions.

But not to me.

My spirit was unsettled and disappointed, even though from the outside it appeared all was well. Inside I was screaming for answers and direction. Every day became full of expectancy. When I questioned God about the silence from other Christians, He simply said you will hear only from me until I'm ready to let others speak into your situation. He told me this way I would not have to wonder about different words spoken to me.

There is no way I can list all the things that God spoke to me over the course of those three years. If you are out there and you feel alone, I want you to know you are not alone. It's okay if no one is calling you out. I've been guilty of running after the church functions, thinking that maybe I'll get a word tonight, seeking some kind of direction. I found out that sometimes just being still and doing the next right thing is a very peaceful place.

In September of 2016, I had a dream while visiting out of town. This one dream was so vivid that even today several years later I can tell it in detail. I was in a room and a preacher and his wife entered the same room. The woman walked over to me and laid her hand on my forehead. She was speaking in the heavenly language, then she began to speak these words to me, "thou are as a woman forsaken."

Waking up from this dream I immediately knew

> *For the L*ORD *hath called thee as a woman forsaken and grieved in spirit, and a wife of youth, when thou wast refused, saith thy God. For a small moment have I forsaken thee; but with great mercies will I gather thee.*
> **Isaiah 54:6-7**

that this word was also quoted in the Bible. I found the scriptures and read them, and then I knew what lay ahead. The Lord was letting me know that I would feel forsaken, but it was only for a season.

Many times the Lord would tell me to praise Him. He would tell me to lift up my voice to Him, to be thankful for the process. So I tried to hold on to faith and kept going to church. But I was just going through the motions of what I thought I was supposed to do.

Yet again, another word came to me in my preparing season. God was keeping me. "You're living in the shadows of your calling," was the word that came this time. Every time God spoke to me I could find the phrase in the Bible. He told me I was abiding under the shadow of the Almighty. He had me covered. He knew that my gifts and calling were being confined. I could see the corner that I was backed into. The beautiful thing about it was that He had me in that corner. He was protecting me from myself as well as others.

I love the story of Joseph in the Bible because he had to go through a process of events before he stepped into the role that God intended for him to follow. He was given a dream about his future, like many of us today. He had plenty of setbacks. I believe every setback was a setup for his position.

A lot of times our roadblocks or our feelings of being mistreated will come from within our own close relationships. Just like the story of Joseph though, every situation can be traced back to God taking us through a process.

I encourage you today to lean on the Lord. Look to Him, no matter how unfair it seems. Joseph was sold by his brothers, lied on by his master's wife, thrown into prison, all on his way to becoming second in command over Egypt and fulfilling the purpose that God had planned for him all along.

"The doors of opportunity swing on the hinges of opposition!"
-Adrian Rogers

He that dwelleth in the secret place of the most High shall abide under the shadow of the Almighty.
Psalm 91:1

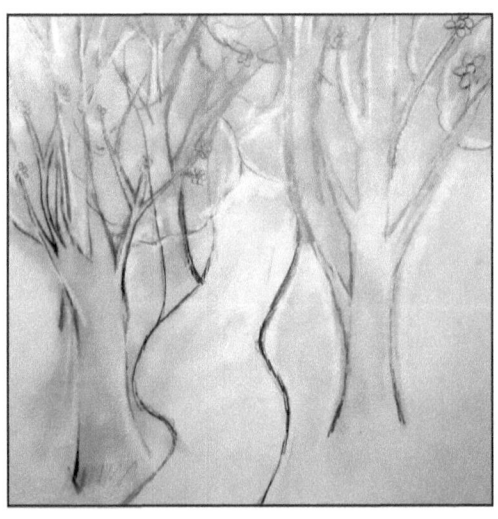

Chapter 4: Shadows

I needed clarity of the prophecy that I was living in the shadows of my calling.

What was this calling? I had to find out. I was on a mission to find this calling, this purpose, and to find my place. Little did I know that I would become a pastor's wife. This did not happen for probably two more years, but in the meantime, the pursuit continued.

During this seeking season, ideas were coming from everywhere. One of the projects that was stirring in my heart was to start a team with some other ladies from the church I attended. We named our group Acts 29, We Are The Next Chapter.

We started in early 2017. We would meet up at different locations, sometimes in my home, sometimes at little eating places. Our goal was to reach out to other women, go to the hospitals, and visit the sick.

We had logo t-shirts and totes, excitement was in the air. Even though the group itself didn't continue, the desire to work did not leave me. I eventually changed the name to Sheila's One Stop and later to Bee Ministries. It may seem like I was involved in a lot of projects, and I was. Because the Bible tells us to ask, seek, and knock. If you will pursue the work of God you eventually will find the right path and find your purpose.

The adventures continued. Me and my husband would pretty much pay out of our own pockets to pursue these dreams and callings. We had a few people investing in us. They believed in us. Our Acts 29 group also hosted a seminar called Brokenness to Wholeness. A dear sister-in-Christ who lost her son a couple years before this spoke at this event. We wanted to do outreach ministry. Many times during this birthing season, we would feel resistance. Often it felt as though the ones we had sweet counsel with were the very ones that would put up the walls, but the resistance became our greatest asset.

God let me know in one of the projects that was on my heart. God was doing so much in me that I wanted to share this wonderful knowledge with the world. We were still in our old church at the time, and I went to my church leadership to get permission to start doing some videos with biblical insights on my Facebook page and on my Acts 29 page.

At first, all was well and the request had been granted. So imagine my disappointment when the answer changed to "not right now." During the counseling, my game face of faith never changed. That night my heart was so hurt. *Why, God?* I asked. The answer was yes, then turned into not now. I was wrestling with these emotions when the Lord spoke to me. He said, "It's not about them. It's about you. You need to learn how to deal with no." Then it all made sense. It was simply part of the journey to our new beginnings.

The battle was raging between God's angels and the devils. My mind often went back to the dream about being a woman forsaken. The Lord had told me, "You will make it through this season. Stay focused, pray, and fast; keep doing what you're doing because this is testing time." This was my strength on many days. Remembering His words kept me going.

We were desperate during this time, doing all we could to find our purpose for the Lord. If you just bear with me, I want to share a few more endeavors that we were doing to knock on those spiritual doors.

We were at youth camp the summer of 2016, and during the night a great idea dropped in my spirit: back-to-school outreach. I reached out again to leadership, and the event was given a thumbs up. So many people came together for this. Donations were coming in like crazy. The date was set. Our church got involved and we were so pumped. We tied our Sunday school service to the event. Prizes were given away along with hundreds of school supplies for the community children. The Acts 29 group began to help pack the bags. Okay God, we were doing something. We were giving of ourselves and our resources. It felt like a software was downloading in my spirit. The passion to find that calling, that sweet spot, was pushing my mind to think outside the box.

After the back-to-school outreach, we immediately began to plan for the fall festival. This was something that our church did every year. Yes, you guessed it, the ideas came flooding in. Let's take this event up another notch. How can we make this an outreach? As always, the donations were there. Hoe Down On The Ponderosa was going to be a success. We built seasonal fall backdrops for pictures. Bouncy houses were rented, little riding barrels were pulled by a four-wheeler. Lots of food and plenty of drinks were available.

It wasn't just a reflection on the church we attended. It simply was part of this journey that was already bigger and better than we expected. Along with just a few other people, my husband and I financed the event, and it was a huge act of faith. It was about helping others and seeing where God was taking us. Hindsight is 20/20.

Don't be discouraged when you have dreams and

visions of doing something mighty in the Kingdom of God, and if those things seem like they are beyond your reach or if you come up against walls like we did, just continue to seek God, continue to pursue the longing in your spirit. You will soon find a door that will open for you. A door of opportunity. A door of destiny.

There will be challenges that will come along beside you. Just know that God is greater than your past. And your past can be forgiven, which gives you the right to walk out your God given purpose.

"The eye is always caught by light,
but shadows have more to say."
–Gregory Maquire

And the Lord answered me, and said, Write the vision, and make it plain upon tables, that he may run that readeth it.
Habakkuk 2:2

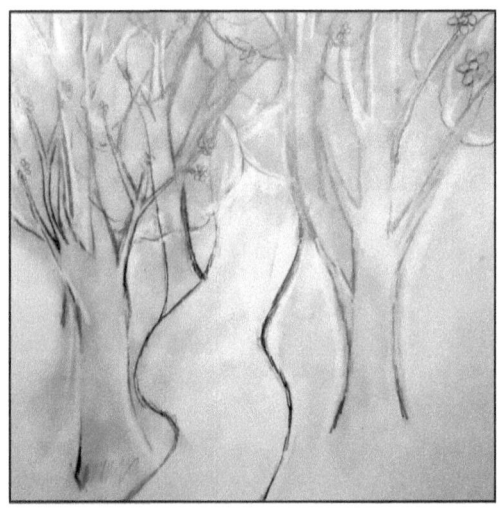

Chapter 5: My Journal

My days were full of great expectancy. As I wrote about in chapter 2, I flew for the first time in 2016. As I flipped back in my journal, I found more pieces of this journey to new beginnings. These events aren't all in order, but they happened as a building blocks to where I am now.

I found in my journal an entry where I had met with a couple of ladies who attended another church. We met to discuss our trip to the conference in Miami, Florida. We were excited to be going to this great event, Women Ministering to Women. I had never flown in an airplane before, but the longing to do something new and outside of my comfort zone was pushing on my heart. The check was written to cover my ticket. Then the planning began; expectancy was in the air.

I didn't know what awaited me there. It was a great chance to see some places I had never seen before. We were on a mission to find ourselves or to find that great call we felt, but there was turmoil in the area.

A hurricane had been on the move before we landed. The place that they had originally rented for the event was shut down, so the service was moved to a hotel conference room. Some of the ladies were not able to attend because airports had stopped flights becasue of the bad weather. This trip would still not give me answers or the direction that I was searching for, but there was value in it for me. The services were intense, and I found great friends and more ladies that were on the same path. The experience was priceless to me.

On June 19, 2017 I wrote, "Your beginnings are small but your latter end will be great." These were some of the words that were being dropped in my spirit at that time. "When I do what I'm going to do, it's going to be so mind blowing, mouth dropping." Again, this was another word God brought to me. On this particular page of my journal, I found some dates that I'd written down. This is where the new me was beginning to form. I started declaring, decreeing, and believing for things to come to pass. By June of 2018, my husband and I would already be walking out our calling and purpose. The things that God spoke to me would come to pass.

As I write this book, the memories are so sweet to my soul. Now, at the time that I was writing out my feelings and uncertainty, it wasn't always glorious. One day at a time had to be my pace. If my thoughts went too far in the future, it would get overwhelming.

My spirit was crying out to God. Everything seemed to stand still for weeks at a time. Then God would move things in the spirit and we would increase the fervency and time spent praying, and our fasting got more intense. We knew things were moving forward, closer and closer to the door that He had shown us.

Can I be brutally honest? These days were very trying to say the least. My prayer time often felt like war. "Bawling, squalling, and kicking the wall," was my saying at the time. I expressed this to some of my close friends, and we had a good laugh because they understood.

It can be so helpful to find a few good friends to go to with all these frustrations, friends that walk with you on this journey. There is nothing like finding a person that can relate to your journey, also one you can trust to not judge you, but someone who will encourage you instead.

My journal kept secret some of my most difficult

times. Never did I imagine that a book would be in my future. One thing about writing on those pages and being able to share raw feelings, it kept me sane. But to know that a book would emerge from it was beyond me.

Let me encourage you today, go ahead and write those things down. We never know what may come from it. Your children or grandchildren may one day read your deepest thoughts long after you're gone. This book started as a desire to share our journey, but as I get further into the writing, the purpose gets more personal. It can be a legacy for our children, a book that can help them when their paths begin to pursue more than what they see with their natural eyes. Habakkuk 2:2–3 tells us to write the vision, write it plain:

And the LORD answered me, and said, Write the vision, and make it plain upon tables, that he may run that readeth it. For the vision is yet for an appointed time, but at the end it shall speak, and not lie: though it tarry, wait for it; because it will surely come, it will not tarry.
Habakkuk 2:2–3

The heart sees a different outcome, but our natural eyes can only see what is before us. My journal, my prayer book, is full of desires and visions that have been put in my spirit. This passage of scriptures is such a great encouragement to me, because it speaks of writing down what our hearts can see, which awakens a new desire to want to move beyond the norm. I will never stop writing down my vision or my desires. My journal will be a place where I can see how I can live out all God has shown me He wanted to do in my life.

If you are not writing down your desires, your longings, your vision of what you would like to see come to pass in your life, then you are missing out on one of the most precious gifts that God has allowed us: to go beyond our natural thinking.

But they that wait upon the Lord shall renew their strength; they shall mount up with wings as eagles; they shall run, and not be weary; and they shall walk, and not faint.
Isaiah 40:31

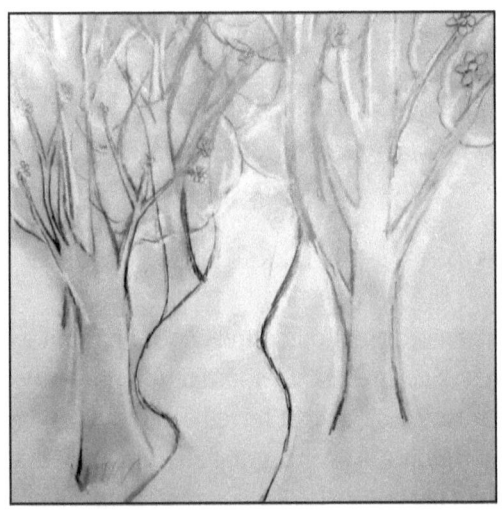

Chapter 6: No C-Section Callings

In August of 2017, a thought came into my mind: No C-Section callings. I called my daughter and began to share this thought with her. A few days passed with much seeking for the interpretation of this message God was laying in my spirit. More verses came during the night hours. It became clear what God was saying to me. I was pregnant in the spirit with a vision. Passion and purpose were breathing down my neck. The birthing process was going to be painful. No spiritual epidurals.

My mind went to the metaphor of a butterfly. Just like the butterfly, the struggle is what brings about the beautiful wings which allows it to fly. I once read a story in which a man saw a butterfly struggling to get free from its cocoon. He thought that maybe he could help it. He took a pair of scissors and cut the hole bigger, and the butterfly came out without any struggle. But as you may have guessed, the wings were not developed. So the butterfly could not do what it was born to do. After a while, it died, never getting to fly.

This thought would not leave me. As the week unfolded, I understood it clearly. A good friend of ours, a neighboring pastor, got in touch with me to come and preach for them. I was glad to be able to minister to this church. I preached for them on several occasions.

One night, God revealed a passage of scripture to me. This time it was book, chapter, and verse, no thoughts, no words. I knew God was ministering to me on a different level.

I felt a little reviving in my bondage. That night, as I was delivering my soul to this beautiful assembly, my husband had fallen really sick and I did not even know. The message was on point and powerful, not because of me but because of where we were on this journey.

> *Declaring the end from the beginning, and from ancient times the things that are not yet done, saying, My counsel shall stand, and I will do all my pleasure:*
> **Isaiah 46:10**

The Lord had given me some insight through the word of God. The Bible often used the illustration of a woman in travail to show people praying and seeking God. I shared with them how the enemy had almost numbed our understanding of these scriptures.

We live in a day where very few women have natural birth. There is an article that I read about cesarean sections in October of 2018. It said that the rate of C-sections was increasing at an alarming rate. Since 1990, C-sections have more than tripled from about 6 percent of all births to 21 percent.

Man has played with mother nature so much that we can almost decide the day and time that our little one will arrive. We work around certain days. Women will sometimes even choose a C-section for convenience. Sometimes this is to preserve the life of the mother and child, but other times it is human meddling.

To compare this to our callings in God, sometimes people will settle for titles and positions. But the quick fix often aborts the real calling. Causing us to miss our true purpose which in time will show up if we are patient.

After the service was over, the pastor's wife told me that my husband was in the truck waiting on me. He was laid back in the seat in so much pain. I felt sorry for him and asked him why he didn't let me know. "You were doing what God called you to do," he replied.

We went straight to the hospital. After hours of tests and waiting, he was put into a room. He had a blood clot in his lung. Three or four days passed by while we were still trying to make sense of the situation. In the physical realm, the problem was in his medicine. Thankfully, it wasn't long before he was released, and they adjusted some of his meds. In this spiritual realm, we knew that our desires were being tested. We believed that it was part of the birthing process for our destiny.

C-sections limit how many times you can give birth. We knew that there were several places God was calling us to. There would be no C-sections for us. We were determined to see this through. Something big was coming and we knew it.

Though thy beginning was small, yet thy latter end should greatly increase.
Job 8:7

Chapter 7: Seasons

We knew that our gifts were being tested. Every person has a gift and a calling. Sometimes it takes pressure to reveal those precious gems. What was this season we were in? Some seasons are harder than others.

I knew the Lord was telling me to dig deeper. It was definitely a time of refining, and I turned to the Bible as my main source of strength during this time. I was able to encourage a few friends as well. This is one of the gifts that God graced me with.

One friend contacted me from another state, asking for my help. The next year and a half would be a great challenge. She was a backslider wanting to come back to God. She was very sick and needed to change the way she was living. Her first goal was to quit smoking. We began to pray for different situations. God knew she needed me and I needed her. We went into spiritual war for her. Many days were spent sending her scriptures. Our messaging app was our new best friend. She wanted to get her own place since she was staying with her daughter. God answered that and each request in the process of time. Really, a book could be written about our journey together.

Sometimes we are looking for platforms to step out on and great doors to open. God is simply seeing where your heart is.

One night I was half asleep in my recliner and for some reason I reached out my hand like I was catching a ball. The name Nona Freeman fell into my hand. This was around September 2017. I had read about Nona in a few books. After a few days, I decided to look her up on YouTube. Several clips of her preaching appeared on my screen. The first one was a message called "Not my will, but thy will be done." Without a doubt, God was giving me a word straight from heaven.

I read that Mrs. Freeman often heard from God at 2 or 3 a.m. She also wrote several books and was an evangelist and a missionary in Africa for many years. I could feel a shifting in my spirit. It felt like a mantle had been dropped on me, which made sense since she was deceased. There is a story of a man of God named Elijah recorded in 1 and 2 Kings. Elijah passed by Elisha and cast his mantle upon him.

So he departed thence, and found Elisha the son of Shaphat, who was plowing with twelve yoke of oxen before him, and he with the twelfth: and Elijah passed by him, and cast his mantle upon him.
1 Kings 19:19

This was a sign that Elisha was going to be Elijah's successor. From that moment on, Elisha followed close to Elijah. Elijah would often tell him to stay behind as he went on his journey, but Elisha would not leave Elijah's side. Elijah asked Elisha what he wanted to gain from following him. Elisha responded to the man of God, I want a double portion of your spirit.

Finding out about Nona Freeman helped me to recognize that God had a greater purpose for me. I felt like it was a pull to seek Him in a deeper manner.

I have learned in my walk with God that He often speaks in the early hours, just before dawn. I would encourage you to pay attention to those early wake up times. In fact, next time you are awakened at 2 a.m. or 3 a.m., ask God if He wants to share something with you.

God ministered to me so often in those early morning hours. I would love for those reading this book to find those same encouraging moments. It will take you to a whole new level.

I pray that after this book, your life will forever be changed. The time that God has given you here on this earth will move forward, and you will be a great asset in His Kingdom.

The battle continued. As I continued to journal and hear from the Lord, my spirit knew that in this season, I had to press on. I regularly prayed for hours a day. I was not a spiritual giant, but I was simply in a time of preparation. So a lot of my days were consumed with reading books. Not just any books, but books that were going to push me through to find my purpose. I also found encouragement online; I spent hours on YouTube listening to spirit-filled preachers and motivational speakers.

During this time, I heard about how different people would seek God for a word for the following year, so I began to ask God for a word. This was in 2017 around September. The request was not just for 2018. My situation needed a word right then! God spoke the word *embrace* to me. I pondered on that word, and God began to show me how to embrace this season. Don't resist the process. Learn from it, grow from it, embrace it.

> *For thou shalt break forth on the right hand and on the left; and thy seed shall inherit the Gentiles, and make the desolate cities to be inhabited.*
> **Isaiah 54:3**

And embrace it, I did. The spiritual downloads were coming almost daily and not uncommonly at around 2 or 3 a.m. "Breakforth on the right hand and on the left. Your season is almost over." Like I've shared already in this book, there were only a few things that God spoke to me that are not in the Bible almost word for word. All these things, your children, your bills, your circumstances, will not move you. Wow, what a beautiful thing God was doing in my walk!

"God is able to turn the tables." As I pondered what this meant, you better believe this girl was rejoicing. I found this phrase meant to refer to a board game or games. If a person is losing and the tables turn, the one who was losing will start to win. My godly morning, my new day, was coming and I knew it. Sweeter was the journey, because this season was appointed unto me. He told me that this test was already aced. The answers were in the book all along, and it was an open book test.

> *Nay, in all these things we are more than conquerors through him that loved us.*
> **Romans 8:37**

The phrase *appointed unto me* is found in the book of Job. I just want to add a little input here about Job. Most people have read or heard of Job at one time or another. He was perfect and upright, that's what the scriptures tell us. He lost his children, his cattle, and Satan even attacked his body. This took place because God was watching him, and He knew Job's heart. God knew Job's walk was more

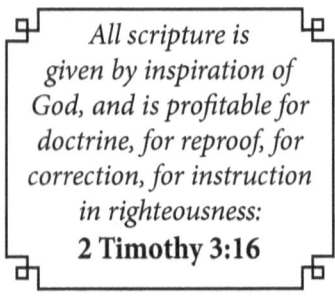

> *All scripture is given by inspiration of God, and is profitable for doctrine, for reproof, for correction, for instruction in righteousness:*
> **2 Timothy 3:16**

> *My foot hath held his steps, his way have I kept, and not declined. Neither have I gone back from the commandment of his lips; I have esteemed the words of his mouth more than my necessary food. But he is in one mind, and who can turn him? and what his soul desireth, even that he doeth. For he performeth the thing that is appointed for me: and many such things are with him.*
> **Job 23:11–14**

than just talk. In the middle of his test he testifies that this trial had been appointed unto him.

In the passage above, Job is speaking to God about his walk with Him. In verse 14, he was saying that God had brought him to this point.

We sometimes think that when trouble comes we are not going to make it. I don't want to just tell you how God had an appointed season for me without giving you an example. Job has been my go-to several times. He can be yours as well. When you feel like you're backed into a corner, you can look to Job. Also, you can reflect back to this book and remember that Sheila went through a season that God appointed and came out with more strength, more direction, more clarity for her journey.

I'm in no way comparing my situation to Job's. My takeaway here is that God is the all-knowing God, and He will keep you in your appointed season.

It was the best of times, and the worst of times. (I've always wanted to use that phrase in a book.) It truly was. The Lord took me to the scriptures for wisdom and perspective in 2 Chronicles 20:12. Jehoshaphat was being attacked by three armies. A letter containing strong compelling threats was sent to him from the enemy. Jehoshaphat went to God and spread the letter out before the Lord.

"Truth. Lord all these things are true, he has done all this to our neighbors. Our eyes are on you only. What else can I do?"

He knew the one true living God. In verse 15, a messenger begins to declare the words of the Lord: the battle is not yours but God's. So we can all look to God in our most trying times and know that He is there.

"People are put into your life for seasons,
for different reasons, and to teach you lessons."

–Selena

Then said he unto me, Fear not, Daniel: for from the first day that thou didst set thine heart to understand, and to chasten thyself before thy God, thy words were heard, and I am come for thy words.
Daniel 10:12

Chapter 8: The Word

The word came. December 9, 2017 will forever be sketched in our hearts. New beginnings, this next year will be a year of new beginnings. I knew I had heard this word from God.

The next few weeks leading up to the new year in the natural world were exciting to say the least. As I began to share my word with close friends, I was introduced to the meaning of numbers. I uncovered that three and seven were among God's perfect numbers. After sharing this on Facebook, a few people responded that the number eight meant new beginnings. Immediately I hopped on the internet for confirmation, and I found a little more information on the reason for the meaning. Even though the year was 2018, all I could see was the eight.

The Bible says that God created everything in six days, then rested on the seventh. After seven comes eight. The new world had started, a new beginning. The number 8 in the Bible represents a new beginning, meaning a new order or creation.

I saw confirmation everywhere as so many new blessings were revealed and new work began. On January 1, 2018, my journal writing was exploding with prophecy, speaking into our future resounding all the things that God had spoken to me. It was also the beginning of our third year since God told me we wouldn't always be there.

June would be the month that would tell all. I knew that change was in the air and we were about to see some things with our natural eyes. The Lord was still downloading His future plans into my spirit. We decided to make a 30-day sacrifice: no bread, no sweets, and no meats.

> *Turn you to the strong hold, ye prisoners of hope: even today do I declare that I will render double unto thee;*
> **Zechariah 9:12**

I remember one of the things God told me. He said when I do what I'm going to do, it's going to be mouth dropping and mind blowing. I kid you not, it came just like that. Ask for double, I'm going to give it to you. This time was no different, I went to the Word to find out what God had intended for me.

Since it was now the year 2018, I wrote down eighteen things that I wanted God to double. During this exciting time, my heart expected harvest. I decided to have a meeting with some other lady ministers at my home. We shared our dreams and goals and traded our written requests with each other, with the purpose of praying specifically for those petitions. I shared with them the prophecy of the new year and the asking for double. I asked them to pray that God would show us where we were supposed to go or what we were supposed to do.

Not knowing it would be my last message preached at my old church, the title that I used for my sermon was New Beginnings. As I planned for my words, I looked for

> *Behold, I will do a new thing; now it shall spring forth; shall ye not know it? I will even make a way in the wilderness, and rivers in the desert.*
> **Isaiah 43:19**

inspiration, and with it being a new year, my emails all seemed to be centered around new beginnings.

This picture came in an email, so with the help of our tech person at the church I incorporated it into the message. Centering the message around this theme and the number eight, I was able to bring the people into the vision that I was encountering. There were several passages of scripture that were very potent for me in this important time.

Several events took place in that first month alone. We got new phones, upgraded after more years than I care to share. The church we attended started MIT meetings (minsters in training), and this was a great learning experience for all involved. My ladies in ministry meeting was in January. Also, my daughter Vanessa Wheeler accepted her calling to preach this beautiful gospel. Being a minister myself and evangelizing when the opportunity came, it made my heart swell. Overjoyed was one of my many emotions in those days.

*For a great door and effectual is opened unto me,
and there are many adversaries.*
1 Corinthians 16:9

Chapter 9: The Building

There it was, the building that would become our church. It happened so fast. We had gone out searching like we normally did on a free Saturday. Today was different. An incredible presence filled our truck. We always held hands and prayed about our endeavor to find that place. Today was different because we were going to a new city. We had searched for several months, but today we took a whole different direction.

The sign said the little red brick building with white trim was for sale or rent. My husband called the number to inquire about the amount of rent. Without even hesitating, my husband said "We want it!" Also, to make the situation even sweeter, there had already been a church in this building. The landlord was out of town, but would return Monday.

Monday came and we got the news he had gotten sick. So you know how we are as humans, we start fretting about the direction. Is this really God? Is this just our desire?

God always has a reason and a purpose for every delay. They finally got to meet that Thursday, and the delay in meeting up was totally a God thing. Remember my number 8, and the meaning? If they had met on Monday it would have been the 5th. As it turns out, the meeting was on February 8th, and I got a picture of my husband holding the key to our new building. When I looked at the date, all I could do was rejoice. The number eight means new beginnings.

To top off our already awesome experience, after hearing my husband's passion and desire for the building, the landlord took a hundred dollars off the rent.

That following Saturday night, we let our home church know that we had found a building and our calling was taking us to a different place.

My husband and I were the only ones there on that first Sunday. We sang and prayed and read a passage of scripture. The feeling of perfect peace was in the air.

The second Sunday, there were eleven of us. Of course, that included our daughters and their children, along with my niece, but it was growth none-the-less. There we were, though, in Blytheville, Arkansas, stepping out in faith.

Today, we are still in that little red brick building. We have about twenty-four members at the time I'm writing this book. There have been times when only eight of us were there. Honestly though, I never have been discouraged. When you get a word from God and you know without a shadow of a doubt that you are in His perfect will, no devil in hell can dampen your spirit.

It was no small stir. People began to send love offerings shortly after we signed the lease for the building. You see, this was not an overnight decision. Many people knew that God had been calling us to do a work. Often, when people would speak of our new church, my reply was it's really not a new church, it's a work that God sent us to. It was born in my soul a long time ago.

In my acknowledgment page I list some of the precious people that gave to us and some wanted to remain anonymous. During the first few weeks, a dear friend of mine contacted me and began to prophesy that we were going to be blessed financially.

Checks were coming in the mail. Big checks. We were so overjoyed to see people sowing into the work.

Looking back in my journal there were many events taking place that had been written down long before. Desires and dreams that we had seen in our spirits. On November 24, 2017, I had written in my journal about a building. My prayer was a prayer of thanksgiving. Through other books and videos, I learned to thank God for what He was going to do. I thanked Him in advance for those promises He showed us. I thanked Him for the people that were already being put in place to sow into the work.

This writing my thoughts down, declaring His promises, and reading them daily was one of my greatest revelations. There is nothing too hard for God. All things are possible through Him. Little did we know what lay ahead for us. We had no musical instruments, no sound system, no pews. God was working to provide. My stepdaughter, Shanda, her boyfriend at the time, and their children all started coming to the services.

My niece lived only a few minutes from Blytheville. She originally attended the church that we left, but because of the distance she had pretty much quit going anywhere. She was there the second Sunday and has been coming ever since. We knew God had sent us.

Shanda and Bryan went and bought a keyboard and drums. She played the keyboard while he played the drums. My husband found a sound system for $150. We were able to do the soundtracks on our phones.

Bryan's uncle, Mr. Latham, runs a funeral home, and he also has storage buildings, etc. Bryan worked at the funeral home during this time. Mr. Latham gave us about thirteen pews. After we got them in the building, we cleaned them up and thanked God for His provision.

Our journey continued, and with each week came another blessing. The first few months were filled with provisions, blessings, and life changing events.

There is one story that I must share because it was such a defining moment in our new path. I had recently become close with a former friend. We had talked in times past and often ended up in the same church services, youth rallies, revivals, conferences etc. But we started to connect on a more personal level.

One morning my friend Natalie sent me a video chat with a word from God. She began by telling me that this word would not leave her alone. Often when God wants her to share something, He will nudge her spirit several times and that was her confirmation to share with me.

The message was simple yet so exciting to hear. God had big things in store for us. She told me that we were going to be blessed over the next few weeks. She said people were going to reach out to us. She warned to not reject the blessings, because God would use his people to show His favor on the work He sent us to do.

I was excited and expectant, and I didn't have to wait long! Not three weeks, not three days, but that very day, it started. I went into the local grocery store, and as I was shopping, a gentleman walked up to me with a coupon for a free ham. He asked if I would like the coupon. He told me he had won it at a work picnic, and that he drove a truck for work, which meant he was on the road most of the time, so he would be glad for me to get the ham.

I wasn't sure what to think, but remembering the word that I had just received, I took the coupon, and of course I thanked him. I immediately began to look at the date and read all the details on the coupon. I took the coupon to the meat department to see if it was legit. The amount was up to $30. The worker told me it was in fact legit. Leaving the store that day, this girl was on cloud nine. Not just because of the ham, but because of the miracle that just took place. I returned the video chat to my friend, letting her know that God was already working.

This only got me more excited. It put my spiritual antennas up. It made my expectancy level rise to an all-time high.

She was right. People began contacting us to ask for our address. Within just a few days, checks were coming in with notes saying that the givers felt impressed to help us with the work of God. Not just little checks. Some were $500! One person gave my husband the money to pay for the rent of the building, not just one time, but for about six months!

We went to different church events, and even there people would give us money. We are still so thankful for all of God's provisions, blessings, and life changing events.

I also want to share a little story of how we believe that God was remembering us for our sacrifice. A lot of people didn't know that my husband sold a gun to get us in the building. This wasn't just any ol' gun. This gun was very dear to him. It was a gun that he had always wanted, a deer rifle I believe. I found out while editing this book that he sold several guns that were dear to him.

My husband wanted to show God that he was willing to do whatever he had to do to move the work forward. He sold the rifle for less than it was worth because he had a passion and desire to step into this lifelong dream he had from a young age: God had put in his heart to pastor a church. Be encouraged today, dear brothers and sisters, in the Kingdom of God, if He brought you to it, He will bring you through it. In a sense, my husband had all but given up on this calling. Because of different circumstances that had evolved in his lifetime, he thought all hope for these callings to come to pass were gone. Here we are today though walking in our callings, obeying the voice of God.

Now I want to take you into the next chapter where faith meets passion.

"Either a building is part of a place or it is not.
Once that kinship is there,
time will only make it stronger."
–Willa Cather

Call unto me, and I will answer thee, and show thee great and mighty things, which thou knowest not.
Jeremiah 33:3

Chapter 10: The Calling

We went to Blytheville for a calling, not just so we could say we had a church. My husband had the call to pastor for many years. Life happened as it often does. Many setbacks and heartaches marked the way along this journey. We had a dream of starting a work, not just a church. Even though we are so grateful for the little red brick building, we know that it's not our final stop.

The city of Blytheville has several vacant buildings. We continue to look for a bigger building. My husband wants to fulfil the call that God placed in his life. He wants to build a Christian school, a place to have events like conferences and seminars. We want to teach people that you can reign as kings and priests for the glory of God.

Price Chopper, the old supermarket building, was one of the buildings that we were drawn to. It was a radical move of faith that was seen by hundreds of people when my husband announced that was the place. We began to go by the property regularly. We would speak to it, pray over it, and then give God praise.

After a few weeks, Kennith began to share his vision of marching around the building like they did around the walls of Jericho. We didn't record it at first, but then we decided to let the public know what our hearts were longing for. Week three, week four, and so on. Facebook was loaded with post shares, comments, all encouraging us. Every week I would go with him and do a Facebook live video.

When people would ask, "Have you got the

building yet?" my husband would simply say, "Not yet." During the weeks of marching around the building, there was great expectancy. We called to inquire about the price. The one million dollars they were asking did not discourage my husband. Every Sunday he would excitedly tell our assembly about the great revelations that God was sharing with him. One in particular was how God told him to go buy this property without money. He sees the amount as no concern to him. He said that God only needs him to believe. So, believe is what we are going to do.

While we are still in the season of waiting, we are continuing to work and reach for the lost souls. My passion to work in the Kingdom continues to burn in my soul. God's timing is different from our timing.

I set a goal to start a ladies' Bible study. God had opened my eyes to so many biblical truths about how to live in perfect peace and victory no matter what was happening in life. He had changed me. My desire was to share that with other women of faith.

I longed to have meetings to share the word of God. We had a few women's gatherings at our new church building, but it did not have a dining area. It's good to have a place to have refreshments and a place to write down information when you have a meeting. We had several ladies who wanted to come as soon as there was a place to come. Most of them were from the area where we were living at the time, so we searched for a place in our local town.

During this time, Kennith worked for a company that was bringing a four-lane highway through this town, which caused him to befriend a lot of farmers and business people. When you are messing with people's yards or land it can get very touchy. God always lets my husband find favor with them.

So, he asked one of his new friends if they knew of a place his wife could hold some Bible studies. He got a little emotional when this man offered him use of a building that would be perfect. We only needed it for two hours a week for six to eight weeks. And again God provided.

Next, I desired to host a ladies' retreat. This new longing was to do something that would make a difference in someone's life. I found that hosting these events made my heart feel full and soul fulfilled, but somehow I felt held back. I was not sure of the resistance that was present. But sometimes God will block things until His perfect time.

With my pastor's approval, the retreat was finally scheduled. We were excited to say the least. Several of my close friends that shared those visions with me helped to bring this event together, making it a very successful retreat. Twenty-five ladies gathered together with one purpose. The God of Second Chances was the theme.

God sees your desires. He sees the longing to make a difference, the longing to fulfil your callings. I know from experience that He will open the doors for you when the time is right. My goal was to awaken sleeping giants in their lives. It was targeted at women that had either failed God before or after they came to know Him. Women who had a bullseye on their back, for those who felt failure, despair, and undeserving of God's great mercy. This retreat was just the beginning of more events to come. This great accomplishment helped grow my faith, expectancy, and drive even more.

Am I doing all that is in my heart? Not yet. But I am working toward those things. Writing this book fulfilled one of the goals that I wrote down on my list. Another project on my list was to start a blog to share these great truths that turned my life around. The blog is centered around a theme that was dropped in my spirit back in 2017. If you could go back to my memories on Facebook, you would see even then that it was a very big part of my way of asking, seeking, and knocking.

      Some people would say don't put your goals or dreams on social media. I agree somewhat to that philosophy, but just as Joseph shared his dreams with his brothers, sometimes we need to share ours. Yes, Joseph was sold into slavery, lied on, put into prison. I don't believe he would have started his journey to be a prince over Egypt without the process. So pray about what you share for sure, because I still have things that I have not shared publicly. But sharing these dreams and goals on social media allows not only me to look back and remember how they came to pass, but it can also show others what God can do. It's a sure way for God to get the glory.

**"When Christ calls a man,
he bids him come and die."**
—Deitrich Bonhoeffer, *The Cost of Discipleship*

Now the Lord had said unto Abram, Get thee out of thy country, and from thy kindred, and from thy father's house, unto a land that I will shew thee:
Genesis 12:1

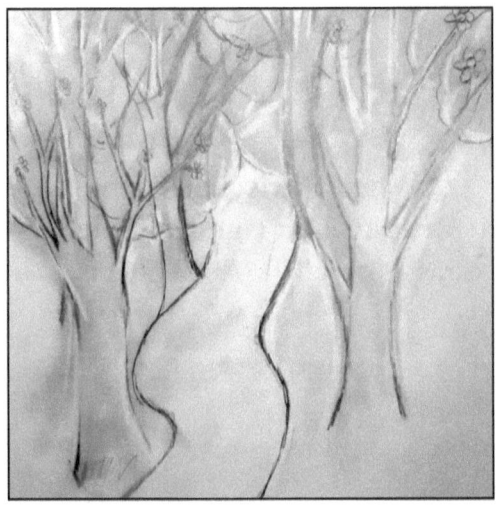

Chapter 11: The Move

We still lived in our former house when we started the work in Blytheville. We rented from our pastor at the time. We loved where we lived; it was big house out in the country. The drive to our new church was roughly thirty minutes, and we desired to move into the city where we started our church.

      A lot of our free time was spent looking for just the right place. So from February to November of 2018, we continued to drive back and forth. Winter was closing in on us, the desire to get moved pushed us forward. While I was heading up the ladies retreat, my phone buzzed with a notification. The picture text from my husband showed a key, with the message 'I found a house.'

      I tried to not overreact about this decision that was made without me, but it had my mind running in circles. One of the reasons we were trying to move before winter was because we burned wood for heat. We loved the wood heat because the electric bill was never high, but it is quite a chore messing with wood. Quite a bit of repairs needed to be done to the older place. It just made sense to move soon.

      "This house is too little," I told my husband. We were living in a twelve-room house, how could we move into a four-room house? But my husband had been praying about the move. He gave the Lord a certain amount that we could pay for rent. The house he found was exactly the amount that he brought to God. The rent in this city was high compared to where we were.

      I have to tell you this little house could have gotten

the owner five hundred dollars per month, easy. The house belonged to a great friend of our son-in-law. They were in the middle of remodeling and were living out of town. Their goal was to sell it. We had met them a few times; we knew God had let us find favor in their eyes.

My husband asked the Lord to provide us a home for only $250 per month. This ask was almost impossible, but nothing is impossible for God. You guessed it! We got it for that!

Packing up and storing lots of stuff was definitely not my cup of tea. Our time to live there was only temporary. We'd still look for a bigger house at the right cost, but this little house got us close to our church before winter. The reason I tell this story about the move, the house, the amount, is because all these events were leading us to our destiny. God is in every detail, weaving provision and blessings into every step.

In March of 2019, I was offered a little painting project. I entered the house that needed painting and just said to the Lord that this is the perfect house, not too big, not too little. Our former house in the country had two huge bathrooms. For many months my request to the Lord was for something smaller than the house in the country, yet still with two bathrooms.

The house was being remodeled for the man's brother. Just that Sunday my daughter's husband preached a message called Building Your Nursery. He brought the message about the Shunammite woman who had a room built for the man of God. She didn't realize that she was building a nursery. She was simply making room for the man of God in her life, but in return she would conceive, bringing forth a son.

Sometimes in our sacrifices of money and time we

are sowing into a harvest.

As I painted the walls, my mind said, 'this is the perfect house.' It was in a great location and surrounded by a great neighborhood. I texted my husband this message, 'I'm painting my nursery.' He knew what it meant. But the owner of the house was set on renting it to his brother. After about a month, my husband stopped by to talk to the owner, who was also a good friend to my husband. Again, the answer was no, his brother was still moving in.

At the end of April, he texted my husband and said he thinks his brother is moving out of state. For some reason, I knew even when I was painting, it was going to be ours. God knew the sacrifice we had made. He knew that my heart longed for something nice. Of course, the rent was higher. Let me tell you though, when God has sent you to do a work, you step out on nothing. You leave all comfort, all sense of security. He will go before you even in the smallest details. The house was offered to us with a hundred dollars taken off the rent. God was going before us and paving the way in every area for this work to which He called us.

My greatest goal in writing this book is to speak to those visions in your life that lay dormant. Our journey continues even as I write this book. We're experiencing divine connections, favor from people that God has brought into our lives. And I believe there will be a next book, because without a doubt God is going to do more than our human minds can comprehend. The building that we are believing God for, the other books, the blog, website, and other endeavors are on the horizon.

I joined the Toastmasters club after I started writing,

and I have also earned a Life Coaching Certificate. The life coaching path began to emerge through the writing of this book. My desire is to help fellow Christians to see that failure is not final, that every bump in the road can be used as a stepping stone to take you higher.

    I will never stop reaching for the stars, because the God of second chances never took away my vision to see more for Him. My blog is called Bee Bible Smart Blog, along with Bee devotionals. Please continue to follow us as we follow Christ into more new beginnings.

The Journey Continues

We are still here in Blytheville, Arkansas in 2021. That little red brick building still accommodates our church services. The pandemic of 2020 took its toll on us as we maneuvered our way through online services to going back in person. We are still holding on and looking to God to see us through. We are not discouraged. Our faith is strong in God and the work he sent us to do.

Several new things have emerged as we moved forward in the work of the Lord. One of them being the Bee Ministries. At the time I'm writing this, I have two Bee Devotionals available on Amazon. I'm working on the third one. My goal is to have 12 devotionals published over the next several years. I also plan to write another memoir, a follow-up to this book.

I have watched God unfold the rose in my life and connect the dots. He has connected me to the right people at the right time. My goal has not changed, even though it has taken on several different forms, from writing books to putting out Bee Devotional calendars and even having some t-shirts made with different bee designs. You might ask, what goal? The longing in my heart to help someone to rise up to their potential. To see others find their God given talents and bring them to fruition. To leave an impact on the world and a lasting memory for future generations.

You can find my devotionals on Amazon, under my name. I have an author's page on their website with all my writings. God bless you all and I pray today that you run after your destiny in Christ, and don't stop till you reach your goals.

In Christ,
Sheila Textor

Acknowledgments

This is a different kind of acknowledgment page. Most people will use this page to thank those who helped them on their journey. Believe me, that will also be included in this page but that's not all.

If you would allow me the pleasure to be a little sarcastic towards the enemy of our souls, I would like to thank him too. His schemes helped to move us forward in the kingdom.

Thanks for every road block, it helped us to learn to seek God for the right turn. Thanks for every mountain that you put in our way, because it made us climb higher.

Thanks for every person that you used against us, because it made us pray more. Thanks for every struggle, because it produced the butterfly that was trapped in that cocoon.

Thanks for every time you attacked our finances, because it only made our faith grow stronger.

Thanks for resistance, because like the airplane it only helped us to fly higher.

There is a lot more I could thank him for, but you get the picture, right?

Now, to truly give thanks to some very special people for their contribution. There are several who wanted to remain anonymous, I honor their request. This dedication page is not only about the book, even though it all helped us get to this point.

Many prayers went up on our behalf. Truly you can't put a price on that kind of help. This journey that I share would not be possible without people listening to God and giving to our ministry. I have asked for permission to share their names in this book and it was granted.

Now the amount is not even relevant. I want to focus on the reason for giving and being obedient.

Brother and Sister Paul Lawrence from Christian Worship Center, may God bless you a hundred times over for what you gave. You sowed a seed into someone else, and that will forever bring you a harvest.

Sister Tina Jordan also from Christian Worship Center, may the God of the universe reach down and bless you exceedingly, abundantly above all that you could ask or think. You gave at a time that you really needed it yourself. That, my friend, will bring a great harvest.

There are several more that God sees and knows about. They already know that God has repaid them above anything they could imagine. One person gave for about six months toward the rent on our church building. Can I tell you that God was moving and supplying for us, we were so amazed, yet so humbled.

Bryan and Shanda Pillow gave beyond anything that our minds could fathom. Thanks so much for all you have done and continue to do. God will not forget your labor of love.

There are quite a few people that gave to us monetarily, gave us spiritual support, and prayed for the work of the Lord to move forward.

For two of the most important people in my life, God and my husband. I want to thank you both from the bottom of my heart. Words cannot express my deepest gratitude. To my husband, Pastor Kenneth Textor, you have been my biggest fan other than God. You have seen my ugly cry, and felt my deepest heartache while I was in this painful process. Thank you for letting me pursue my heart's desire. Thank you for letting me quit my job that was part of our income. Thanks for never discouraging me from pursuing the writing of this book. The pages couldn't hold my gratitude toward your kindness. You have got to be one of the most selfless people that I have ever known. I say to you, my dear sweet husband, we have only just begun to see the great and mighty works of God in our lives.

    To my God and savior of my soul, thanks for stretching me beyond my comfort zone. Thanks for the growing season. Thanks for giving me back the years that the cankerworm stole from me. Thanks for giving me back my tomorrow when I threw tomorrow away. Thanks for showing me what I could be and where I could go with you. I know that the pages in this book cannot even hold what you deserve. But I know that you are my everything. I'm forever grateful for your love, grace and mercy.

www.ingramcontent.com/pod-product-compliance
Lightning Source LLC
Chambersburg PA
CBHW030909080526
44589CB00010B/219